Books by Joseph F. Dinneen

WARD EIGHT

PIUS XII: POPE OF PEACE

YANKEE FIGHTER
(by John F. Hasey, as told to
Joseph F. Dinneen)

PURPLE SHAMROCK: JAMES
MICHAEL CURLEY OF BOSTON

ANATOMY OF A CRIME

UNDERWORLD U.S.A.

QUEEN MIDAS

THE ALTERNATE CASE

THE KENNEDY FAMILY

THE KENNEDY FAMILY

THE
KENNEDY FAMILY

by Joseph F. Dinneen

with Illustrations

Little, Brown and Company
Boston · Toronto

*Published simultaneously in Canada
by Little, Brown & Company (Canada) Limited*

PRINTED IN THE UNITED STATES OF AMERICA

TO MY WIFE
Helen

FOREWORD

For more than twenty years it has been my assignment to cover Joseph P. Kennedy and to keep an eye on his growing family.

What he said and did in Boston or away from it was of particular news interest in the city where he was born and raised. I interviewed him often in his progress to prominence, from the time when he was the youngest bank president in the country to the time when he served as Ambassador to the Court of St. James.

As his sons and daughters grew older, they too made news, not entirely because their father was a millionaire, but because what they said and did was, very often, interesting.

At the same time, as an observer of the Boston political scene, it was part of my business to follow and report the career of James Michael Curley as Congressman, Mayor and Governor — and the Kennedy bête noire. As his biographer I became familiar with the details of the long cold war between Curley and three generations of Kennedys.

In this narrative, I refer occasionally to "a reporter" or "the reporter"; in these instances, I am usually referring to myself.

J. F. D.

Illustrations

THE KENNEDY FAMILY

❧ I ❧

JOHN FITZGERALD AND ROBERT, the brothers Kennedy, are products of wealth, determination and a peculiar political heritage. They have never known financial insecurity, and barring the conquest of the United States by a foreign power or the complete collapse of its economic structure, they never will. Joseph Patrick and Rose Kennedy, their parents, begot a large family. In the course of time it has become an organization dedicated to one purpose, the election of John F. Kennedy to the Presidency of the United States.

Joseph P. Kennedy, one of the richest men in the country, if not the world, is prepared to spend his last dime to achieve that end if it appears that his son has a fighting chance.

Three generations of Kennedys have lived according to a tradition established by Patrick Joseph Kennedy, widely known as "P.J." and more intimately as "Pat," who was born in East Boston in 1858, some twelve years after the

3

great potato famine in Ireland. He was intelligent, sharp, shrewd, quick to recognize an opportunity and make the most of it, the type usually described in obituaries as "a born leader." As he saw it there was room for only one at the top. A contender who placed second was a loser.

He began as a dock roustabout and longshoreman in the days of the Knights of Labor, parent organization of the American Federation of Labor. He was good-natured, generous, popular and careful with his money. He got around, making friends and influencing people, and inevitably became ward boss of East Boston.

Before the turn of the century, he had acquired enough money to buy a couple of saloons and a coal business and establish the Columbia Trust Company in Maverick Square, the East Boston business center. He moved his family into a fine house on Jeffries Point, East Boston's equivalent of Back Bay. His bank thrived, arranging mortgages for the longshoremen, dock workers and Democrats who bought houses in the less desirable areas of the ward, and in time he opened a branch in downtown Boston. Pat was softhearted, but never to the point of not foreclosing on delinquent mortgagees.

His reputation was one of utter honesty and fairness. Although he dealt with politicians such as James Michael Curley and John F. Fitzgerald in the days when Boston was first becoming "a horrible example of graft and corruption," Pat managed to keep his reputation unsullied and beyond criticism, quite a feat for a member of a company of five political kingmakers who hand-picked governors and mayors. Pat did everything right, at least as far as the public record and the recollections of the city's oldest inhabitants go.

He married Mary Hickey, the right woman to help him make a happy, comfortable, profitable and full life; they had three children. He set a pattern of behavior for his family; his son and daughters adhered to it strictly themselves and transmitted it to their own children and grandchildren. The code might have read as follows: "Come in first; second place is failure. Don't make mistakes. Do nothing that will reflect upon your moral character or reputation for honesty and integrity." It was and is a code requiring rigid discipline — or superior discretion.

Top spot, first place in political or public life, does not mean governor of a state or United States Senator; it is the Presidency of the United States.

Pat would not have contemplated it as a goal in his day, nor could he have foreseen a time when a Catholic might aspire to it. He was concerned only with ward, city, and state matters. He had a head for figures, whether they were election results or bank deposits. He served in both branches of the state legislature, the House of Representatives and the Senate, but he was far more effective as a manipulator behind the scenes.

The son, Joseph P., inherited his father's natural gifts, enhanced to a greater degree. He exceeded his father as a politico-financial genius to become a stock market speculator with extrasensory perception, a soothsayer who could foretell what stocks and bonds would rise or fall and how much either way. Although never a candidate for public office himself, he surpassed his father as a backstage strategist. He learned how to make money, but he also learned how to spend it efficiently and effectively for political purposes. Franklin Delano Roosevelt testified to that after his first campaign for the Presidency.

In the epic of the phenomenal Kennedys, Patrick J. Kennedy, important as the original architect of the family structure, has long since been overshadowed by the results of his creation.

Pat, in his prime, was about five feet ten inches tall and weighed about 185 pounds. He had a sandy complexion and blue eyes, and cultivated a luxuriously curled mustache, a vogue of the day. A close friend once summed up his way of life for a reporter thus: "Sure! Pat sold liquor, but he was a dutiful Catholic who never raised his voice in anger or used profanity."

At the turn of the century, he was chairman of the "Board of Strategy," a group self-constituted to pick all Democratic candidates for city, county and state offices, dictate appointments and generally supervise patronage. Three members of this board have sunk into oblivion — their stories are inconsequential footnotes in the city's history. For the record, they were James Donovan, chairman of the Democratic City Committee, Joseph J. Corbett, judge of the Land Court, and W. T. A. Fitzgerald, Register of Deeds.

The fifth, an unrelated John F. Fitzgerald, was to play an important part in the political training and education of Joseph P. Kennedy and his children. He was known variously as John F., Fitzie, Honey Fitz, Little Nap or The Little General, depending upon whether he was being introduced at a political rally, singing on a stage or in a club, or caricatured in a Democratic or Republican newspaper.

Fitzie was undersized, much shorter than Pat Kennedy, about five feet two inches tall. He was always smiling, dapper, debonair and wore a boutonniere — the archetype of New York's Jimmy Walker in a later day. He was a wit and a wag, quick and ready with a flip retort. Politicians despised him, but the voters loved him.

He was a sports enthusiast, a familiar figure at championship bouts, a rabid baseball fan, leader of the Red Sox Royal Rooters in whatever city they played a crucial game. He would sing "Sweet Adeline" in a melodious tenor voice in any park, arena, theater, living room or front parlor. He had physical courage and once aroused became a cocky, fighting bantam rooster. He once sallied with fists flailing into a company of college boys who had pelted Richard Gerard, the composer of "Sweet Adeline," with ripe vegetables and fruit.

Throughout his long political career he was the world's foremost song plugger for that tune. As an unofficial goodwill ambassador he sang it before the crowned heads of Europe and in South American countries. Years later, when President Franklin D. Roosevelt made state visits to cities south of the border, he was serenaded with it; it seemed that many South Americans thought "La Dulce Adelina" was the American national anthem.

Fitzie was his own greatest admirer. He claimed credit for whatever was accomplished while he was in any public office whether he had a hand in it or not. One of his severest friends and best critics summed him up at a banquet

7

in his honor this way: "Fitzie discovered Niagara Falls, conceived the High School of Commerce, built City Hall Annex, invented political ether, put an end to the Spanish and the First World Wars, planned the Chamber of Commerce, freed Ireland and invented the Ku Klux Klan to save the Irish from being bored in America."

In contrast to Fitzgerald, Pat Kennedy achieved prestige and dignity. Along with the politicians, voters, applicants for jobs and supplicants for aid who filed through Pat Kennedy's house week in and week out over the years, Fitzie was a regular visitor. Pat privately characterized him as insufferable. They did not get along too well, but they needed each other. Pat could not banish him, abandon him or make him disappear. At the turn of the century, he would have shuddered at the thought that both of them would one day have grandchildren in common.

Joseph P. Kennedy was born on September 6, 1888. He came into the world with a heritage of talents in two fields, politics and finance. His father was then a member of the state House of Representatives. When Joseph was in kindergarten, his father was a state Senator. Throughout his childhood and formative years he was constantly in an environment of politics and finance.

He attended the Church of the Assumption parochial grammar school where the nuns gave him particular attention, not because his father was rich and prominent, but because he was an exceptionally gifted pupil — they discovered in him almost immediately a phenomenal aptitude for mathematics. He became absorbed in problems, intent

8

upon solving them, curious to find the answers and fascinated by the science. The nuns were good psychologists — they did not set him apart or hold him up as a shining example; he got no special treatment.

Outside of school, he became a strict conformist. He sold newspapers not because he had to, or because he needed the money, but because all the other kids in the neighborhood did. Boys who were poor by comparison were his chums, and he played baseball and football with them on the mud-flats. When he was in the seventh grade, his parents took him out of Assumption School and enrolled him in Boston Latin School to prepare for Harvard.

This was an unusual thing for Irish parents to do. Most Irish children of that era, even though they had no prospect of going to college, were taught at their mother's knees to hate Harvard and cheer for Yale or any other opposing college team. Besides, Catholic young men and women were expected to go to Catholic colleges — if they could afford it.

At Boston Latin School young Kennedy attracted almost immediate attention for the same reason as before, a prodigious propensity for mathematics. The late Patrick Campbell, who later became superintendent of the Boston schools, was then teaching the subject there and discovered the boy's talent. Two kindred souls with a common interest, they became fast friends. Campbell probably did more to shape Kennedy's career than any other person, and until Campbell died, Kennedy consulted him often. Away from the city, he was likely to call him long distance to discuss complex financial problems and factors involving stock market operations. Whenever he returned to Boston, he never failed to visit him.

While attending Boston Latin School, Kennedy played basketball and baseball. He loved competition and lived up to his father's rule that a Kennedy must come in first — a rule that would be honored by the procession of Kennedys to follow him. If the team lost, he was bitterly disappointed. If it won, and he did not have a decisive part in the victory, he was still disappointed. At the end of his senior year, he won the John F. Fitzgerald Mayor's Cup for the highest batting average in the Boston high schools.

There was some irony in this award. Fitzie had no voice in the choice of a winner. He merely donated the prize. He stocked cups for all sports and all occasions. If beauty contests had been popular in his day, he would have stocked cups for those too. He thrived on publicity, and a cup got his name and sometimes his picture in the newspapers.

Pat Kennedy and Fitzie, almost of an age, were contemporary officeholders. Like Pat, Fitzie had served as a Boston city councilor and state Senator, but unlike Pat, he had departed for four years to serve two terms as Congressman, although he came home from Washington as often as he could to attend the meetings of the Board of Strategy.

Two terms was enough. Fitzie was homesick and out of his depth in national affairs. He felt that he knew how to run the city, but not how to run the country. He wanted to become mayor (a charter change now provided a four-year term) and was concerned about another rising young politician who might become a serious threat to him. He had first met James Michael Curley in Pat Kennedy's house and from the moment that each saw the other and shook hands, they were instinctive enemies.

Pat was impressed by Curley. He had served in the City Council, as a representative in the legislature where he distinguished himself as a tough fighter, a good debater and a dependable public officeholder who, once committed, honored his agreements after election, discharged his obligations and paid off on the line. As between Curley, tall, broad-shouldered, now emerging as a powerful public speaker, a good vote getter, with his Tammany Club and the Roxbury wards in his pocket, and Fitzgerald, a political clown, a buffoon song and dance man, Pat was inclined to pick Curley.

The other members of the Strategy Board were not so sure. They knew what they had in Fitzie. He had served one term (1906-1907) as mayor. Curley was an unknown quantity. He could very easily take the bit in his teeth and run away with them. It was finally agreed that Fitzie would become mayor and Curley would go to Washington as Congressman.

This guaranteed Fitzie the first four-year term. He was making his bid for it when young Joe Kennedy won his baseball cup, and it was a foregone conclusion that Fitzie's second term would be a repetition of his first, and consist of his seeing the world, singing "Sweet Adeline," entertaining and enjoying himself.

During his first term, he took his family abroad with him, entered his daughter Rose in the Sacred Heart Convent near Aix-la-Chapelle where she studied music and

French and German until she could speak both languages fluently. She had been graduated from public schools in Concord and Dorchester High School. The voters back home thought that he might stay there until she graduated, but he returned in time to embark on his own campaign for the second term.

Rose Fitzgerald and Joe Kennedy were not strangers to each other. Rose was a very pretty girl. She was the apple of Fitzie's eye and he delighted in taking her around with him, showing her off at parties, banquets and balls and at political rallies and meetings. Even in the days before women had the vote, it was good technique to demonstrate that he was a proud and affectionate father.

The Kennedys did not visit the Fitzgeralds, except on special occasions, but political protocol required Fitzie to call upon Pat when pots were simmering. He usually came accompanied by Rose. Joe had an eye for an attractive face and a shapely form. He and Rose had a good deal in common. She had been brought up in a similar environment, and their experiences had been almost identical.

The same kind of visitors came to her house as to Joe's week in and week out — politicians petitioning for favors or support, applicants for jobs, supplicants for public welfare. She and Joe had heard the same pleas, the same proposals, the same arguments, the same voices echoing through their houses in anger or anguish. Whatever situation existed between Fitzie and Pat, whether they were temporarily close in agreement or friendship or momentarily at swords' points could not affect Joe and Rose.

They could be friendly and unconcerned regardless of the transient differences of their fathers. Pat and Fitzie must have been aware of the growing friendship between the young people. Joe squired Rose about to dances and the theater. Whether their parents approved or not, they did not interfere.

In 1908, John F. Fitzgerald was inaugurated Mayor of Boston for the second time; his daughter Rose went abroad again to tour the Continent, improve her piano technique and advance and broaden her education. While there, she became an avid collector of the autographs of kings, queens, princes, princesses, lesser royalty, the famous and the prominent; meanwhile Joseph P. Kennedy graduated from Boston Latin School with honors and entered Harvard.

Joseph's restless spirit would not permit him to keep quiet. He must always be doing something — he could not loaf. During the summer months he worked as a candy butcher on the Boston-New York boats merely for the satisfaction and enjoyment of making money. Having fun during vacations was an energetic business, too. Whether swimming, horseback riding or playing golf, he did it as vigorously as though he were out to break records. All of his children share this characteristic.

Harvard Coach "Pooch" Donovan considered Joe potential professional baseball material and tried to teach him to slide to first by whipping his legs with a rope or swiping his head with a wet towel. How this would accomplish the intended result seemed to be Donovan's secret — at any rate it did not work. Classmates recall Joe's last play in the final game of the year with Yale. Kennedy, at first base, caught a hot grounder, made the last putout and walked off the field with the ball in his pocket. More than forty years later, his youngest son, Teddy, would do something like that in football. In the final play of the Yale game, Teddy caught the ball as it bounced off a goal post, depriving Yale of its last chance.

While still a student, Joe demonstrated that he had a King Midas touch. For a quick business venture with ready profit, the sight-seeing buses at Boston's South Station attracted him. With a college mate as partner and a shoe-string for capital, he acquired them. Boston bankers and businessmen who later looked upon Kennedy with awe must have passed him when he wore a black and white-visored cap as he tried to persuade strangers to see Paul Revere's house, the Old North Church, Lexington, Concord and other points of interest. The two boys did this for three summers while they were in college, and at the end of that time Joe had $5000, which in that day was more than an average new college graduate would make in a year. Joe had long since determined that he would one day be a millionaire.

During Joe's sophomore year, Rose Fitzgerald returned to Boston after two years abroad and resumed a political and social round as the Mayor's official hostess — her mother was too shy to play much part in breaking champagne bottles on the bows of battleships at launchings, sponsoring concerts and visiting settlement houses. She was appointed a member of the Public Library Investigating

Committee assigned to determine what books children should read. It soon became obvious to their friends, moreover, that Joe Kennedy and Rose Fitzgerald would one day be married.

Joe Kennedy always knew what he wanted, and he never hesitated over a decision. Immediately after he graduated from Harvard, it was no trick to have his father obtain an appointment for him as State Bank Examiner. That was what Joe wanted. There was purpose and method in his selection. It gave him an opportunity to look into the businesses and practices of banks. It would reveal the sound and solid and the shaky among them and it would make him known personally to all bankers in the city and state.

It irked the bankers to know that the son of a business rival had access to their books and to discover that he was capable of analyzing their businesses, but they could do nothing about it. It took the young examiner only a matter of months to find out what he wanted to know. There were a number of bank combinations in Boston in 1913, and Joe could anticipate what was likely to happen. He got his father and relatives together, gathered $45,000 from them, bought the stock of the Columbia Trust Company just before the outbreak of World War I, and his father emerged as president. Joe succeeded him, at twenty-five years of age — the youngest bank president in the country.

Joseph P. Kennedy and Rose Fitzgerald were married on October 7, 1914, in the private chapel of the Archbishop's House in Boston by His Eminence William Cardinal O'Connell. Less than a score of persons, chiefly the immediate families, were present in the small chapel. Best man was Joseph Donovan, Harvard '11, a close personal friend of Joe. After a two-week honeymoon, the couple returned to make their home on Beale Street in Brookline.

ᥰ᛫ 2 ᛫ᥰ

THE DISTINCTION of being the youngest bank
president in the United States may have pleased Joe Kennedy, but it was far from the realization of his ambition.
His goal was higher than that. He had hardly warmed the
chair before he set about making a series of mergers and
consolidations. He began by reorganizing the Collateral
Loan Company.

He violated the staid traditions of the dignified Beacon
Hill moneylenders and abridged a few ancient canons and
time-honored customs by going directly to the core of a
situation instead of discussing it interminably with the
conservative Boston financiers before acting. They looked
upon him with suspicion as an inexperienced, brazen up-
start, doomed to failure. The reorganization of Collateral
Loan was an unqualified success, but that did not change
their minds about him.

For his part, he looked upon them as a company of
senile, timid veterans, hidebound and slow-moving. His experience with them would color his opinion for the rest of

his life. Speaking before a Chamber of Commerce group after he had moved his base of operations to New York, he told them: "Boston is a good city to come from; but not a good city to go to. If you want to make money, go where the money is."

His operations in Boston reverberated in other cities and money markets. His name was becoming known. Charles M. Schwab had heard about him before he met him. The United States was tooling up for war in 1915. It was clear then that the country soon might be drawn in. Officer Training Camps were in operation. Cantonments and camps were being planned and built. More and more bright young executives were persuaded to get into war work.

Schwab, then president of Bethlehem Shipbuilding Company, invited Kennedy to discuss joining his staff. They met and Schwab asked him to become assistant general manager of the Fore River Shipbuilding Yards in Quincy, Massachusetts. Kennedy thought it over and accepted. This brought him in contact with an Assistant Secretary of the Navy, another Harvard man and former editor of the *Crimson*, Franklin Delano Roosevelt; the two became close friends, and their association was to prove fruitful for both of them.

Kennedy's rise in the world of finance was interrupted meanwhile, or at least limited, for the duration of the war.

John F. Fitzgerald had lost an election and gained a son-in-law. It had been agreed by the Strategy Board that Fitzie would relinquish the office at the end of his first four-year term. Curley anticipated fulfillment of the promise, but Fitzie and Pat were now close friends, and Fitzie had changed his mind. He decided to run for the third term. Pat Kennedy approved and the Strategy Board went along with him.

Curley was furious. He had expected a shoo-in nomination and election; instead he had to fight for both. The campaign was a bitter one. Every ward leader in the city was opposed to him. He had to fight, sometimes literally, every inch of the way. Accompanied by his strong-arm Tammany gang from Roxbury, he invaded every precinct, faced belligerent crowds at rallies that often broke up in fist fights and proved to be a master of the hostile audience.

When they booed and serenaded him with raspberries as he stood up in the back of an open car, his eyes blazed, his jaw jutted out and he addressed them in the language of the street corner.

"You're nothing but a bunch of doormat thieves, second-story workers and milk-bottle robbers," he bellowed at a crowd in Andrew Square, South Boston, and his voice was heard. A man in the front rank called him an unforgivable name. Curley vaulted from the touring car, clipped him on the point of the jaw and the rally broke up in a riot. Police were called but were not able to restore order. As his car was about to be driven away, Curley pointed his finger at the voters and snarled: "You'll hear me if I have to break every skull in the ward. I'll be back here tomorrow night."

He knew his people. He was a far better psychologist than any ward boss or member of the Strategy Board in the city. The next day he was the talk of the ward in every saloon and barroom in South Boston.

The people loved a fighter, and Curley knew it. True to his word, he was back the next night at the same corner. The voters gathered around silently. There were no catcalls or boos. He apologized for his behavior on the previous evening and asked: "What else could I do? Would you take it if you were in my spot?"

They were smiling now and shaking their heads. This time he turned on the charm, the oratory. He was the poor boy who had helped to support his family, been self-educated, fought his way up against unbelievable odds and was now taking on the city's well-oiled political machine, the rich and the corrupt, trying desperately to overturn a system that kept them poor and downtrodden. He was their sole salvation. They were puppets in the hands of Ward Boss Jimmy Gallivan. Curley would show them what he could do for them after election.

He made converts that night and more on succeeding nights visiting the ward. Similar episodes occurred in every other ward in the city. The Strategy Board and ward leaders knew they had a lion by the tail. Their followers were deserting. Martin Lomasney, described by Lincoln Steffens as a surprisingly honest and intelligent ward boss, defected and went over to Curley.

When the votes were counted, Curley had won in a landslide. The power of the ward bosses, with the exception of Lomasney, was broken. Never again would they achieve the eminence they had hitherto enjoyed. Fitzgerald and Pat Kennedy were retired almost into oblivion. For the first time, Boston had a city-wide boss. In later years, Fitzgerald ran for Governor and United States Senator. He was defeated each time — Curley would have no part of him.

Curley had a long memory. It might have helped to explain, years later, his shoulder-shrugging irritation at any mention of the Kennedys and the cold-eyed disdain with which the Kennedys viewed Curley.

The defeat of Fitzgerald and the election of Curley marked the end of an epoch in the history of the Irish in Boston and the beginning of an era of wonderful chicanery and political black magic: the games of "Now you see it, now you don't!" or "Button, button, who's got the button?" that Curley played with the population of a city and state.

One of the first things the new Mayor did after taking office was to fire or demote every Fitzgerald worker in the city employ. Two obscure city employees, one a meter-gilder in Public Works who worked in a constant temperature of 76 degrees, another, a custodian of the Franklin Park Aviary where a constant temperature of 80 degrees was maintained, were transferred to "The Mile Road" in South Boston to dig a trench outside the Pumping Station in the middle of January when the temperature was eight below zero.

Twenty-two years later in 1936 a Boston writer, covering Curley at the State House when he was Governor, was asked by the editor of *Harper's Magazine* to write a critical piece about him. The reporter recalled a scene from his childhood: his mother in a basement kitchen, crying, praying and wringing her hands as a pneumonia crisis was impending for her husband and her eldest son, the meter gilder and the custodian. He acknowledged his bias and suggested that he was not the person to do the article. "Perhaps you're better qualified than anyone else," his editor suggested.

The writer ran a scalpel through Curley's record, exposing it to public view. The article was said to have been responsible for Curley's defeat by Henry Cabot Lodge for the office of United States Senator. Curley sued the writer and the magazine for a half million dollars damage.

Ex-Governor Joseph B. Ely stepped forward and pleaded for the privilege of defending both. He wanted no fee. He said he wanted only to get Curley on a witness stand in order to ask him a few pointed questions. The offer was accepted, but Curley heard about it and the suit died aborning.

An old grudge had come home to roost.

James Michael Curley's victory over John F. Fitzgerald signalized the arrival of the Boston Irish to full political maturity and sounded the death knell for the departed Brahmins who had ruled the roost in Boston and Massachusetts for two centuries. While Curley was about to be inaugurated Mayor, David I. Walsh was being inaugurated Governor of the state — the first Irish-American Catholic to reach that office. For close to half a century now, mayors and governors, with few exceptions, have been Irish-descended Catholic Democrats.

It also marked the beginning of the decline and fall of the Yankee Brahmin financier and the rise of a new crop of men of money, the third generation of Irish, fresh, vigorous and successful, nudging aside the old and the seedy on State Street and throughout Boston's financial district; Joseph P. Kennedy is himself an example.

The Irish inherited the Boston earth from the Puritans and they must soon, in turn, bequeath it, just as unwillingly, to their own successors. The cycle that began with Curley has all but run its course. To understand why requires some historical background.

The Boston Irish, always so designated as a distinctive breed, although, in truth, they are little different from Irish descendants anywhere else, have come a long way since the colonial days of 1688 when Goody Glover was hanged as a witch on Boston Common for telling her beads and saying the Rosary in a strange and unidentifiable language — Gaelic — while kneeling before a statue of the Blessed Virgin. She also made the sign of the cross and said her prayers in Latin. This, according to Governor Thomas Hutchinson, the great historian of that era, was incomprehensible.

As the first American Catholic martyr, Goody was charged with being in league with Satan. Out of this grew the curious New England legend that all Irishmen were devils who had horns and tails, a belief that persisted for almost two hundred years.

The Boston Irish were a problem even in that day; there were too many of them. Both men and women were constantly being brought to this city by the English settlers as indentured servants — slaves, in effect, until they could buy or otherwise achieve freedom (easier for men than women). They had a passion for sticking together and organizing that the colonists could neither prevent nor control. There were no Catholic churches in the city, but the Irish were stubborn and resourceful and managed to buttonhole French missionaries, traveling through the city on their way South, and persuade them to stop long enough to say Masses. They were a constant irritant and exasperation to the Puritans.

There are old Irish, although not necessarily Catholic, names in Boston, of families who came here soon after the *Mayflower*. The early Irish hated servitude just as ardently as they hate it today. The bondsmen chafed at their bonds and broke away from them one way or another. The indentured women were just as unhappy and more often than not were freed, peacefully or violently, by the Irishmen who married them. By 1737, there were so many Irishmen in financial difficulty in Boston that they organized the Charitable Irish Society, still active and going strong more than two hundred years later.

There were a good many anonymous Irishmen who participated in the Boston Tea Party. The Boston Irish fought at Bunker Hill and at Lexington and Concord. They had far more reason than "taxation without representation" to feel bitter toward King George and England. When the war was over and they tasted the sweets of freedom and democracy, their attitudes changed. They became tradesmen and artisans and ardent champions of civil rights, some of them successful enough to hire newcomers from Ireland as domestics and coachmen.

The size of the Catholic population in Boston gave the Yankees and Brahmins some concern during the first half of the nineteenth century. They were colonizing in the less desirable neighborhoods, building churches and parochial schools, importing and training priests and nuns. Their congregations were tough and rugged, resentful and likely to become pugnacious when pushed around. Yankee blue-bloods then had the money and the votes and fought among themselves for control of the city and state. The Irish looked on and learned.

Boston's best people got the money without personal risk to themselves in a three-cornered transatlantic trade, shipping Medford rum to African ports, picking up slaves there and transporting them to New Orleans where they picked up cargoes of molasses to be delivered in Boston to make more rum. They shared in the guilt for one of the world's greatest crimes.

These early American financiers were astute and crafty. They could not bear the thought of having their fortunes dissipated after death by profligate sons or daughters, and many, therefore, left them to their heirs and assigns in ir-revocable spendthrift trusts in perpetuity, restricting each successive heir to $5000 per year, for example, a tidy sum more than a hundred years ago, but now characterized as "peanuts." The fortunes grew and the funds piled up, but the amounts paid to heirs never could be changed; the Su-preme Court so ruled. There are men walking the streets of Boston today who appear seedy and down at heels even though they are technically part-owners of large slices of the city. The trustees who handle these estates are often paid five times as much and more.

Boston had a well-contained, reasonably law-abiding

Irish population, estimated at ten to twelve thousand in 1848 when the Irish hordes began to pour into the city to escape the devastating potato famine in Ireland. They came as well to Nova Scotia, New York, Philadelphia and any Eastern port open to them. Among them were the parents, grandparents and great-grandparents who would change the face, body and political philosophy of the city. Such men as Patrick A. Collins, Martin Lomasney, Kennedy, Fitzgerald, Curley and Walsh, along with the parents of William Cardinal O'Connell and Richard Cardinal Cushing, sons who would build more churches, grade and high schools, academies, colleges, seminaries and hospitals to establish tradition today's generation follows.

The great numbers of immigrants swelled the city's population too quickly to be readily assimilated. They colonized first along the waterfront and over a period of fifteen years formed a semicircle around exclusive Beacon Hill. They were longshoremen, ditchdiggers, day laborers, human bulldozers, marshaled by the thousands to level Boston's hills, fill in its ponds and narrow its rivers to create living room for themselves and profit for the Brahmin financiers who rented the jerry-built tenements on this made land that became Boston's slums — now century-old eyesores.

They were obstreperous, belligerent when aroused and hard to handle, yet they were kind, sympathetic and generous. They were clannish, congenital joiners. The Sons of Erin and the Ancient Order of Hibernians flourished. They were courageous — they had to be; they were unpopular and discriminated against by the native Puritan and

Yankee stock, for their numbers were becoming frightening.

When the War Between the States came, there were enough Irish immigrant volunteers to fill two regiments, the Fighting Ninth and the 28th, both authorized to carry the green flag of Ireland abreast of the Stars and Stripes. Colonel Thomas Cass, whose statue is now on the Boylston Street side of Boston Public Garden, died of wounds at the Battle of Malvern Hill. Colonel Richard Burns of the 28th Regiment was killed at Cold Harbor.

In addition to its heroes, the Boston Irish had the average quota of conscienceless jokers, the "bounty jumpers" among the sincere bounty men. If a conscript called up for service could find a substitute to take his place, he could stay home and attend to his business or otherwise enjoy life. The federal draft law provided $300 per man. A life was cheap. The jokers sold themselves several times over merely by deserting and finding another prospect for a substitute. Both heroes and bounty jumpers were killed; Confederate bullets were not discriminatory.

The Irish penchant for organizing developed into a genius for politics. First of the great ward bosses was Martin Lomasney — a Boston legend. He met his countrymen as they disembarked at the wharf, herded them to his Hendrick's Club in the West End, found jobs for them and living quarters. He saw to it that they became citizens, fed them and clothed them and never took a penny from one of them. His payment came from the contractors who put them to work. His only other requirement was that they register as Democrats and vote as they were told.

Martin was blunt and honest with the politicans to whom he sold their bloc votes. There was a desperate need for a ward boss like him in that day and he satisfied it. Lincoln Steffens, the great muckraker, author of *The Shame of the Cities*, came to Boston to expose him and remained to respect and praise him.

"Who do you think you're kidding?" Steffens reports Martin asked when they first met. "You get paid for muckraking and I get paid for creating what you call the muck. You have your price and get it. I have mine and get it. You work your side of the street and I'll work mine." From that point they became fast friends.

Before the turn of the century the Brahmins had the money, but the Irish Democrats had the votes.

When James Michael Curley emerged as the youngest candidate ever elected to the Board of Aldermen, ward leaders paid little attention to him. They considered him as one of those inexplicable political accidents, but not for long. He became something of a nuisance at meetings of the Board.

At the end of his first term, they acknowledged that he had "the gift of gab." He made good speeches, but he was too brash and bumptious and they decided to whittle him down to size by defeating him. On the day after election, though, they were confounded. Curley's sun was rising. They could not know it, but it was not to set for sixty years. Within ten years he was a power in the city, a phenomenon in politics. He had an impish skill in creating dissension, setting one ward leader against another.

For a half century he dominated the city and for a short

time the state. He changed the topography of the city and the contour of its coastline. He is responsible for more improvements than any previous ten mayors of Boston. He built schools, hospitals, playgrounds, parks, public roads, baths, municipal buildings, libraries, a zoo and an aviary.

He had a golden voice and could charm the birds out of trees. He could soothe or arouse any audience. He was quick-witted and entertaining and could change the mood of any gathering at will.

He was unpredictable and mercurial. He could be kind and generous, strip off his expensive coat in zero weather to drape it about a derelict, stuffing a five-dollar bill into his hand, and return to his office to ruin a political enemy. He was loved and hated with intensity. He had contempt for the Boston Brahmins and showed it plainly. He had a photographic mind and a fantastic memory. He could quote yards of Shakespeare and recall immediately a speech he had delivered ten years earlier and quote it verbatim.

He was both a horrible example of graft and corruption and the most efficient administrator the city ever had. He was a kind and devoted husband and father. He suffered the trials of Job without complaining. His first wife died, and, at the time of his death, of his nine children only two survived, one of them a Jesuit priest. Perhaps it is fitting that he should ring down the curtain on the Boston Irish political cycle.

The Boston Irish, exposed for more than a hundred years to the influence of bluebloods and Brahmins, soaked up their manners and customs, aped and imitated them. Blue-blood society, with smaller and smaller families, is dying out; the *Social Register,* once a heavy tome, has shrunk to the size of a book of poems. The Debutantes' Cotillion is not what it was fifty years ago. Today the presentation of Catholic debutantes to the Cardinal Archbishop in the Sheraton Plaza attracts far more attention in the newspapers.

The late Cardinal O'Connell and the present Cardinal Cushing have adjured their congregations against limiting the size of families, but to no avail. Whatever happened to the large families like those of the Curleys and the Kennedys? The Boston Irish, too, are vanishing.

The second great immigration wave came at the turn of the century from Italy, Poland and Lithuania. Boston now has a heavy population of first-generation Americans born from those countries, the majority from Italy. For the past quarter-century, the Irish-Americans have had the money and the votes. They still have the money, but they are fast losing the votes. It is significant that the present Governor of Massachusetts is Foster Furcolo.

✄ 3 ✄

FROM THE BEGINNING the Joseph P. Kennedys were an efficiently organized family. There was never need for Joe to be a handyman, puttering around the house, or for Rose to be concerned about cooking or washing. They could afford domestic help. Rose managed the household and the family. That was her responsibility. Joe was free to think and plan. They entertained often, but their house in Brookline also doubled as a home office.

Joseph P. Kennedy, Jr., was born July 25, 1915, not in Brookline, but in Hull, a summer resort town on the South Shore not far from Boston. Children came fast in the Kennedy household. Five arrived within the first six years. Joe walked the floor with them and took them out in their carriages. On one occasion he pulled Joe Junior around the block in a homemade box sled, became preoccupied by his thoughts on how to make a million, and forgot the sled behind him; a stranger found Joe Junior happily gurgling in a snowbank.

Kennedy resigned as president of the Columbia Trust

Company early in 1914; on April 6, 1917, when the United States declared war upon Germany, he was assistant general manager of the Bethlehem shipyards at Fore River.

This fact was a disappointment to James Michael Curley, now a wartime mayor facing an upcoming election campaign for a second term. He needed patronage of a particular kind, places where he could tuck away rising young politicians and fund-raisers between the ages of twenty-one and thirty-one for the duration of the war. A shipyard, of course, was ideal for this. If young men could be placed in jobs essential to the war effort and acquire sufficient training before their draft numbers were called, they could, with the help of friendly management and co-operative draft boards, gain exemption. All his protégés, however, were turned down, at the shipyards; a second Kennedy had arisen to thwart him.

When the war ended, Kennedy remained with Bethlehem Shipbuilding Corporation for a while. Ships were still needed to replenish the merchant fleets decimated by submarine warfare. But throughout the war and its aftermath, he had never lost touch with the stock market; it fascinated him.

He tried to sell Galen Stone of Hayden, Stone & Company of Boston and New York a contract for Fore River to build ships for the Atlantic, Gulf and West Indies lines. Stone was chairman of the board. Joe went to New York to see him, but Stone refused to grant him an interview. Joe lay in wait for him, got on the same train that was taking him to Boston, sat down beside him and outlined his proposal. Stone turned him down; nevertheless within a couple of weeks, Kennedy was manager of the Boston office of Hayden, Stone & Company.

He remained with the company for five years, from 1919 to 1924, long enough to learn all he needed to know about the stock market. He became a fabulous lone-wolf operator riding up the bull market throughout the 1920s, although he never had all of his eggs in one basket. He had an eye for other speculations that he felt sure could be arranged for his advantage and profit. They required risks, but he was willing to take them.

From there on, Kennedy's rise was meteoric. He backed a motion picture, *The Miracle Man,* and got back $3,000,-000 on a $120, 000 investment; and, almost before anybody knew it, Kennedy was in the movie business with control of a chain of thirty-one theaters in New England, and very soon he was in Hollywood dealing in millions.

Talking pictures were coming out of the experimental stage. A scientist named Lee De Forest had perfected a tube using a pinpoint of light to form a track on film synchronizing sound with motion. The amusement business was looking up. Kennedy bought into a small New England chain of theaters early in 1925. Before the end of the year he was on Broadway. Investors in FBO (Film Booking Offices of America) asked him to look over their operation and reorganize it. Within a year he had made it one of the largest producers and distributors of motion pictures in the world, servicing seven hundred of the largest theaters in the United States.

He combined this organization with the Keith-Albee-Orpheum vaudeville circuit and became chairman of the board. At the same time he became business adviser to Pathé Film Company and First National Pictures and brought them into an alliance with Radio Corporation of America, General Electric and Western Electric, under which alliance all of the amusement enterprises he directed would have first call on all new developments in sound reproduction, synchronization and television.

This deal completed, he called Rose at Hyannisport, where he had bought a summer place, and told her to leave the children with Grandpa Fitzgerald and hustle to New York where they would take the *Ile de France* to Europe. He wanted to look over theaters and motion picture houses there with a view to booking American films and vaudeville into theaters throughout the Continent. He returned early in 1929, to become one of the film production giants of the day, along with Zukor, Goldwyn, DeMille and Lasky.

All of this was only part of Kennedy's over-all operation. He was still the lone-wolf speculator riding up the bull market, but in August, 1929, he surprised and disconcerted the Street by selling, converting and clearing himself out of the stock market — weeks ahead of the crash. He gave no reason for it. It was said that he wanted to channel more money into the entertainment industry; that he was lucky; that he had a premonition or was otherwise unhappy about the market.

"How did that come about, Joe?" a reporter asked him years later.

"Very simply," he said. "I dropped in at a shoeshine parlor on Wall Street. The boy who shined my shoes did not know me. He wasn't fishing for information or looking for a market tip. He was the average wage earner or salaried employee playing the market like everybody else in that day. He looked up at me as he snapped the cloth over my shoes and told me what was going to happen to various stocks and offerings on the market that day.

"I listened as I looked down at him, and when I left the place I thought: 'When a time comes that a shoeshine boy knows as much as I do about what is going on in the stock market, tells me so and is entirely correct, there is something the matter either with me or with the market and it's time for me to get out,' and I did."

On Thanksgiving Day in 1955, sitting in the dining room of the big Kennedy house in Hyannisport overlooking the tiny harbor, Rose Kennedy recalled those years.

"At that stage," she smiled, "we were happy to pile our growing family into a Model T Ford every Sunday and Joe would drive ten miles to Winthrop to visit his parents.

"We were living in Brookline then," she explained, "and Joe was usually away, always busy trying to expand the family income to keep up with our expanding family. On pleasant days I took the children for walks. I wheeled one in a baby carriage and two or three toddled along with me. I made it a point each day to take them into church for a visit. I wanted them to form a habit of making God and religion a part of their daily lives, not something to be reserved only for Sundays.

"They were still young and Joe was away for weeks at a time; in the motion picture business in California or New

York. The children who were old enough attended public school in Brookline. We could then afford a governess for the older ones and a nurse for the youngsters. I did not want to move each time Joe changed business enterprises because I thought it was wrong to interrupt school, their friendships, and the routine of the family. I felt the same way when it became necessary to move to New York.

"From the beginning, I tried to avoid the causes of friction among a large family of children. If they have their own bedrooms, their own toys to play with, and their own belongings, they are not likely to quarrel about them. Members of any big family know that a single bathroom will cause disputes. We always had at least three. We had two boats with enough room to accommodate all of the children. When we first came to Hyannisport, we had one large boat and named it *The Ten of Us*. When Teddy was born we bought another and named it *One More*.

"Having a large family is a more interesting experience than any other that I know and it ought to be viewed that way. It's quite a challenge. Children are interesting. No two of them are alike. You have to tend to the roots as well as the stems and slowly and carefully plant ideas and concepts of right and wrong, religion and social implications and applications.

"I kept a card catalogue of my children, recording when each had measles, whooping cough, chickenpox or any of the children's diseases. I made a record of each physical examination and the result and of each visit to a dentist.

"I made it a point always to be home at mealtime, particularly in the late afternoon and evening because children are tired then. The nurse and governess — the cook and domestic help — were tired, too. At lunch time the older children sat at a big table. Two of the little ones sat at a small table. At dinner time the younger ones would eat in the nursery and the older ones might eat at different times. In any case, mealtime was the place for family discussions that sometimes led to arguments. Just as in any other big family, the children might surreptitiously punch or kick each other under the table. That was never too disturbing. If children do not become adjusted in one year, they will the next.

"The children argued about everything and among themselves in sports and games. They were taught to ski, play tennis, to swim and play golf. One of the chief problems for parents of large families is to keep the children occupied, particularly during the holidays. We always had a program prepared for them. They raced against one another and as a family team against others on foot, in swimming and in boats during the summer.

"Throughout the school year they had the same interests and engaged in the same sports as children in our neighborhood. We always lived in a house near a good school and a good playground. It was our idea that if they had to do something, they ought to learn how to do it well in order to compete with children in the neighborhood. All of them went to dancing schools and they began when they were quite young.

"I always felt," Mrs. Kennedy went on, "that if the older children are brought up right, the younger ones will follow their lead. It was easy for all of the children to look up to Joe Junior because he was a good scholar, a good athlete, and popular with girls as well as men in every neighborhood where we lived."

Father and mother exacted a pledge from the children that they would not smoke or drink any alcoholic beverage until they were twenty-one. The incentive was a gift of $1,000, not nearly so important to any of them as being able to say truthfully that the pledge had been kept. Joe Junior was not only meticulous about keeping the pledge himself but he saw to it that all of the rest obeyed it.

By 1926 Joe's base of operations had shifted to New York. The domestic situation changed also when Joe moved his family that year from Brookline to Bronxville, where he had bought a big house. He was home every night now, instead of only on weekends. Rose knew when to expect him for dinner and whether he would bring guests along with him and how many, but this comfortable scheduled, timetable home life could not last very long either. In 1930, Franklin D. Roosevelt was emerging as a front runner for the Democratic nomination for President.

Kennedy liked Roosevelt. The feeling was mutual and had grown stronger since they had worked together during the war. The market was struggling to recover after the collapse. Joe had the time, money and the inclination to join the team trying to nominate and elect him. At that time he had had eight children: Joe, born in 1915; John F., 1917; Rosemary, 1919; Kathleen, 1920; Eunice, 1921; Patricia, 1924; Robert, 1926; Jean, 1928. Edward would arrive in 1934.

Joe discussed the nomination and campaign with Roosevelt in Albany and at Hyde Park. Roosevelt was glad to have him and welcomed him aboard. Joe became one of Roosevelt's close advisers before and during the Democratic convention in Chicago and he accompanied him on his tour of the country after his nomination.

His friends on Wall Street, bankers and financiers in Boston, looked askance at him. It was inconceivable to them that a successful market operator and a millionaire would approve or even tolerate the philosophy of Roosevelt or the social reformers surrounding him; some thought of him as having all but embraced Communism.

It did not occur to them that Joe and Rose had been, from childhood, so deeply involved in the principles of the Democratic party that they could not desert to the traditional party of big business. Joe went all out for Roosevelt without reservations, even though it meant an occasional association with James Michael Curley, who joined Roosevelt in June, 1931, literally by breaking and entering. He barged into Roosevelt's compartment while both were on a train from New York to Boston. Roosevelt was then on his way to meet Colonel House, wartime adviser to Woodrow Wilson; Curley was returning from a grand tour of Europe with his children.

There are conflicting versions of what happened during this strange interview. Curley, hitherto a loyal, enthusiastic Al Smith supporter, said that he agreed to desert Smith and suffer the scorn he knew would be heaped upon him by Massachusetts Democrats to promote Roosevelt's candidacy, not only in Massachusetts, but throughout the country. He would do this before the 1932 Democratic Convention in Chicago, and after it if Roosevelt were nominated, in exchange for Roosevelt's promise to make him Secretary of the Navy.

Both Roosevelt and his son James later denied this, but it is a fact that Curley did risk his political future on what was then a wild gamble. The following day, standing on the lawn of Colonel House's place at Manchester-by-the-Sea, facing a corps of reporters and newsreel men, to the delight of Roosevelt and Colonel House and the consternation of a company of powerful Democrats, including Senators Marcus Coolidge and David I. Walsh of Massachusetts, Curley publicly abandoned Alfred E. Smith and announced for the first time Roosevelt's candidacy.

"Ladies and gentlemen," he said. "We have been making history here today. Franklin Delano Roosevelt is the hope of the nation. His splendid administration of the affairs of the Empire State makes him outstanding as the man to nominate for the Presidency."

Massachusetts Democrats could hardly believe their eyes and ears. They branded Curley a renegade and a traitor and took oaths that they never again would vote for him for any office. Smith had been and still was the most popular figure in the state. Henceforth, Curley was shunned by the Boston Irish. His name was stricken from the rosters and membership lists of their societies, including the Ancient Order of Hibernians, hitherto among his most faithful supporters. He was booed and heckled wherever he went.

Oddly enough, there was one lone but courageous politician who approved and supported him — John F. Fitzgerald, his old archenemy. The two buried the hatchet and became friends.

It is true that Curley bought time on the air, preaching the gospel of Roosevelt; that he conspired to make his way into the convention in Chicago, with the aid of Mayor Anton Cermak, as Jaime Miguel Curleo, chairman of the Puerto Rican delegation, stationed immediately behind Massachusetts.

It is true that when Al Smith failed to win on the second ballot and the "Stop Roosevelt" movement took shape, Curley met with James A. Farley and Louis McHenry Howe, Roosevelt's top strategists, in smoke-filled Room 1502 of the Congress Hotel, from which Curley telephoned William Randolph Hearst at San Simeon and persuaded him to have William Gibbs McAdoo release the California delegation from John Nance Garner and deliver its vote to Franklin D. Roosevelt. That started the landslide.

It is true that Massachusetts Democrats, particularly the Boston Irish, did a complete backflip, and when Curley returned from Chicago received him as a conquering hero and became his obedient servants again.

It is true that during the campaign for election, he delivered a hundred and forty speeches in forty-one days, traveling ten thousand miles by plane, train and automobile, covering twenty-three Western and Midwestern states and that it cost the national and state Democratic committees nothing. He paid his own expenses. He said he spent $185,000 to help elect Roosevelt, although there is no record to support the statement.

Joe Kennedy managed Roosevelt's tour of the country.

He was the executive in command, assigning quarters to the staff on the special train and in hotels, arranging meetings with Democratic leaders in key cities, setting up press conferences; he was quiet, efficient, the man to see before meeting the candidate, but otherwise unobtrusive in the background.

Kennedy was the fly in Curley's ointment. Curley looked upon him as a boy wonder, grown up; a block off the old chip, P.J., and hardly a man to have private and ready access to Roosevelt's ear. There are hundreds of pictures of Curley and Roosevelt, taken when he came to Boston on the tour, but none of Curley and Kennedy together.

Roosevelt appreciated Curley; he recognized him as an ardent and dedicated worker. He acknowledged what he had done and was thankful for it, but Curley was fast becoming his most painful embarrassment. Kennedy accepted Curley for what he knew him to be and ignored him. Curley found ways to bypass Kennedy during the Boston stop. He stepped boldly into a private elevator taking Roosevelt to his room, reached into his pocket and pulled out $2000 in tens and handed it to him.

"You'd better put that away for your own use," he said. "I know what campaign committees are like. They never give the candidate enough pin money. You might see something around here that you'd like to buy."

Roosevelt blinked and frowned. "Thank you, Jim," he said, "I appreciate the spirit in which it is offered, but really, I'm well fixed for money. I'd suggest that you turn it over to the campaign committee."

Massachusetts polled the largest vote for Roosevelt that

it had ever given to a candidate for President. Curley behaved as though he had wrought the nationwide result singlehanded.

Two weeks after election, Curley went to Warm Springs to see the President-elect. He was accompanied by his daughter Mary. He said he met Roosevelt in the study of "The Little White House" there. Missy LeHand, his secretary, Mrs. Anna Roosevelt Boettiger and Roosevelt's personal physician, Admiral Grayson, were with him. According to Curley, this is what happened.

"Roosevelt," he said, "was smiling, cheerful, genuinely glad to see us. He inquired about our trip down and put us at ease, and then we got down to business.

"I suggested some months ago, I reminded him, that I'd like to be Secretary of the Navy and I told him that I hadn't changed my mind and went on to say that Secretary of the Navy had become something of a Massachusetts prerogative. Charles Francis Adams, the present secretary, I continued, is a Massachusetts man.

"Roosevelt agreed at once. He turned to Admiral Grayson and invited him to shake hands with the new Secretary of the Navy and Grayson and I shook hands."

Except for Mary Curley, none of those present could recall any such conversation.

Curley and his daughter returned home and he made it known that he would be the next Secretary of the Navy.

Repercussions were quick and widespread. The suggestion that Curley with his long record of investigations and scandals in Boston (including a jail term for taking a civil service examination for a constituent) might become a member of the President's cabinet, with power to award multi-million dollar contracts for battleships and such, was repugnant to Democratic and Republican critics alike.

Nevertheless, Curley appeared confident that he would get the appointment.

❦ 4 ❧

CURLEY AND HIS DAUGHTER went to Washington for the inauguration. When it was over, he got in touch with the White House and arranged an immediate appointment. The President greeted them cordially that afternoon and came right to the point.

"Jim," he said. "Secretary of the Navy is entirely out of the question for you."

Curley protested, but the President would not be interrupted. "No amount of discussion or argument can change my decision," he said. "I will not go into the reasons. As a matter of fact I have today sent to the Senate the name of Claude A. Swanson for confirmation as Secretary of the Navy."

Curley was disappointed and his blood pressure was rising.

"How about Ambassador to France?" Roosevelt offered him a consolation prize.

Curley thought it over grimly. "That's not for me," he decided. "When I was in France two years ago, Ambassa-

45

dor Edge told me that it cost him $225,000 in excess of his salary to run the embassy. I haven't got that kind of money."

The President shrugged his shoulders, contemplating Curley.

"How about Ambassador to Rome?" Curley asked. "I think I'd like that. I'd be the first Catholic ever appointed to the post."

Roosevelt thought it over, "Come back tomorrow, Jim," he said.

Curley and his daughter taxied back to the Mayflower Hotel. Could it be, Curley wondered, that Joe Kennedy was advising the President? The thought rankled. The White House called and notified him of the hour of his appointment.

"How about the appointment to Rome?" Curley asked the next afternoon.

Roosevelt shook his head, "There have been objections," he said.

"By whom?" Curley asked.

"By Cordell Hull of the State Department, by the King of Italy, by Premier Mussolini and by the Vatican," he was told. "It is unanimous."

According to Curley's oft-repeated version of the episode years later, he had discussed it with Cordell Hull, who had no objections, and he had had the foresight to cable the King, Mussolini and the Vatican and had received answering cables that all approved, and he threw these cables in Roosevelt's face.

There is nothing to substantiate Curley's story. Cordell

Hull denied that he had discussed the appointment with Curley and it strains credulity to believe, apart from the time differential between Washington and Rome, that all three impressive figures would have answered Curley's cables within twenty-four hours.

The following day, according to Curley, he was again called to the White House. Roosevelt greeted him cheerfully, as though nothing had happened.

"Jim," he said, "I've been making a search of the whole country for a man to send as Ambassador to Poland, and I've decided that you're the man who possesses the courage, the experience, the tact and ability to fill that post. Everything is now all settled and lovely. I want you to go as Ambassador to Poland."

Curley swallowed hard, "Poland?" he said, "You want me to go to Poland! That's a job you ought to give to some Republican, or to some enemy you want to get rid of. I haven't been your enemy. I've been your friend." And he walked out.

Curley left Washington a bitter man and a Roosevelt-hater. He got nothing for his time, effort and money, but he capitalized upon Roosevelt anyway. He returned to Boston to announce that he would be a candidate for Governor. He rode into the office handily on Roosevelt's coattails and for two years harassed him for appropriations and funds, and perhaps got more than most governors for WPA, PWA and state-level alphabetical agencies of the New Deal.

Kennedy went back to private business, the movies and the stock exchange, but he did not stay long. Four months after Roosevelt took office, he called upon Kennedy to organize a newly created Securities and Exchange Commission. Kennedy was not particularly happy about it. The stock market had been out of hand. He knew what was wrong with it. His assignment was to contain it; to provide a set of rules that would restrain speculators, frauds, cheats and long-distance telephone salesmen; the grifters and pitchmen who defeated the so called Blue Sky securities laws by operating across state boundaries and victimizing the uninitiate and the innocent.

There were those who thought that Roosevelt had picked the wrong man for the job. But Kennedy knew his way around the stock market and he was familiar with every trick of such unscrupulous promoters, and no doubt with some that they had never learned. He tore into the whole problem with a vicious energy that stunned and bewildered Wall Street.

The biggest racket in the country at the moment was that of oil royalty salesmen, who were stealing millions from gullible investors who had never seen an oil well or an oil field and took the word of a man on a telephone. They had no idea of what they were buying and were chagrined to discover that they had purchased blue sky.

The Securities Act itself did much to restore the confidence of investors, but Kennedy, as an administrator, did more. He went after offenders from border to border and coast to coast. He could identify many of them and had a bird-dog instinct for sniffing out the rest. No longer could they hide behind state laws. He had a federal whip in his hand and used it freely.

As a policeman of the stock exchange, he enjoyed himself and acknowledged it. "You know," he said then, "when I took this job I told the boss" — Roosevelt — "that I didn't want to tie myself down or take on work that would be more than temporary, but I must admit I do get a kick out of it. You can't do the job in a minute or a week, and I don't know how long I'll be here. There is always something interesting turning up. Let me give you an example. I had a prospectus submitted to me the other day by a company applying for a registration of a new issue of securities. Everything was as it should be, but when I read it I noticed that under the company's by-laws its policies could be controlled by a majority vote of the stockholders present at meetings and not by a majority of all stockholders. I threw it out. I wanted them to take me and the commission into court to decide whether we had jurisdiction. I thought it would be interesting to air the whole thing in public. They wouldn't do it. I won without a contest, but I was disappointed. I would have enjoyed the fight."

The chairmanship of the Securities and Exchange Commission brought the members of the Kennedy family together again. Joe went to Washington, hired Marwood, a twenty-five-room house in Rockville, Maryland, about twenty-five miles from Washington, and his instructions to his friends were: "If you come here, be sure to bring a bicycle." Eight of the nine children were with them. Joseph Junior was now a sophomore at Harvard. The rest were in high school or lower grades.

Marwood was busy, both as home and office. Visitors

came day and night and the telephone always was ringing. Eddie Moore, Joe's secretary, who had been secretary to Fitzie when he was Mayor, lived there. Rose and the children spent the winter in Palm Beach and Joe commuted by plane.

Joe arrived at the old Interstate Commerce Commission offices on Pennsylvania Avenue at 8:30 every morning — an early hour for Washington workers under any administration — dispatched his mail, met the members of the Commission at 1 P.M.; had luncheon served for them in his office at 1:30. They adjourned at 2 P.M. and he spent the rest of the afternoon in conferences with heads of divisions and representatives of stock exchanges, banks and investment houses.

Two of Kennedy's four commission associates were from New England: James M. Landis of Cambridge, a former Harvard Law School professor, and Robert Emmet Healey of Vermont, former chief counsel for the Federal Trade Commission, who had conducted investigations into the power interests throughout the country.

Counsel for the Commission was former Judge John J. Burns of Belmont, Massachusetts, an associate professor at Harvard Law School, one of Kennedy's close friends. The Personnel Officer, who passed on all applications for employment, was Captain Joseph R. Sheehan, Harvard '10, who had grown up with Joe on the East Boston mudflats.

Kennedy had been offered other appointments by Roosevelt and turned them down. He said he had no desire to be a public officeholder. He accepted the appointment to the

SEC because, he said, the market was one thing that he really understood.

The purposes of the Securities Act of 1933 and the Securities Exchange Act of 1934 were to correct common abuses that had crept into the system and had been accepted for years. The function of the Commission was to provide as soon as possible a system under which investors could be given reasonable assurances that the representations made to induce them to invest their money were truthful. To do this, Kennedy picked out three hundred and fifty experts across the country and marshaled them to describe, define, explain and detail techniques that were legal, although fundamentally misleading — or in some cases downright dishonest. These had to be eliminated, controlled or governed to make sure that the blue sky could not be sold henceforth under any device and that an investor would be given a square deal and be told all of the facts with nothing hidden before he risked his money. Chiefly, Joe was after the peddler of crooked securities, but he was just as interested in the twilight zone between them and the legitimate finance and investment houses.

His acceptance of the appointment had puzzled Wall Street. He could be favorable to the speculators, they thought, because he had been one of them, or he could be unfavorable for the same reason. He knew from experience what was wrong and when it became apparent that he meant what he said about correcting wrongs, they became his severest critics. They abhorred reform and had fought all bills aimed at achieving it. They had resented and re-sisted the Securities and Exchange Act and the establishment of the Commission.

They argued that neither Kennedy nor any group of men associated with him, including his stock market police force across the country, could make the act and the Commission created under it effective without destroying the country's economic machinery and at the same time indefinitely delaying economic recovery. What they did not seem to realize was that the country's economic machine had already stalled on the White House steps when Roosevelt took office, declared a moratorium and closed the banks.

Kennedy's retort was that the uncertainty of investors resulting from the market abuses had created a log jam in the capital market. He proposed to break it within a year and limited himself to that much time in office. The whole proposal was looked upon with suspicion.

When Kennedy took over the job in July, 1934, he succinctly summed up his career to that point and his philosophy in these words: "Any success I ever achieved was in administrative work and not in market operations. Of course, I know something about the Exchanges, and my experience is that money made in speculation is negligible in amount when compared to the returns received by those who invest their money in securities that have a future and hold on to them. Few who know the facts will deny the accuracy of this statement."

From the beginning, he bore down upon "boiler shops," the sales offices of brokers in questionable securities who use the telephone to "contact" customers with high-pressure talk, operating on a schedule of one prospect sold or given up every three minutes. In a modified form this activity still continues. It has been impossible to stamp it out entirely.

Kennedy was forty-five years old then, looked like a student and wore the horn-rimmed glasses that fascinated cartoonists, but he talked like the man in the street; he used the same emphatic and descriptive language that still characterizes him, words that he never learned at Harvard.

He made it plain at the outset that authorization of an issue of stock by the SEC did not mean that "approval" had been given to such stocks or bonds but only that the issuing companies had complied with the law in filing a true statement of condition. He pointed out that even under the act, an entirely disreputable company could issue securities as long as all of the facts in its prospectus were correct. "There's never any need to rush to buy a security," he counseled. "There's always time to ask someone who knows about it. Competent advice is always available at any well-established house. Above all, there's never any need to buy a stock over the telephone." A quarter of a century later, the advice still stands.

Kennedy took the job as chairman only because it offered a challenge that intrigued him. Within ten months of his allotted year, he had converted most reputable financiers to his side. In May, 1935, there were from six hundred million to possibly a billion dollars in new financing in the offices of lawyers and accountants across the country, almost all of it in refinancing — very little of it in new issues — and new financing usually follows refinancing.

After the log jam had been broken, popular fear was that the market might dam up again, but that did not happen. Kennedy explained then that the market becomes logged only when security prices get too high; when conditions are uncertain and people become afraid. The securities legislation not only restored public confidence but it made honest men out of some of the shady dealers. They reformed and went straight, chiefly because it was good business to do so.

Kennedy's final act, before quitting, was to go after the oil royalty racketeers, beginning with the top operators across the country. State Blue Sky laws could not reach them because they operated across state lines and in some cases moved so quickly that they were gone before state authorities knew they were working. As a federal agency, the SEC could move just as swiftly. Its agents had authority and the equipment to jump the racketeers.

In 1935, Kennedy characterized the phony oil-well racket as one of the biggest in the country. "It is stealing untold millions of dollars from the gullible who buy the stuff on the say-so of some salesman. They've never seen oil fields. They don't even know what they are buying, but still they fall for it." Some of the rackets he eradicated have been revived and survive in a modified form — these very oil royalty and telephone salesman rackets, for example.

When Kennedy resigned, he acknowledged that he "did get a kick out of it. There was something interesting every day." On his final day, as he left the SEC office, he said to his associates: "I'd hate to go out of here thinking that all I have done is to make some changes in accounting practices." The years since have established that he did far more than that.

Outside of his work, then as now, his one compelling interest in life was his wife and children, and it was his intention then to quit public office for good so that he could devote more attention to them. Circumstances at times made it impossible for all of the Kennedys to live in Washington. Circumstances, it seemed, always were making it impossible for the family to be together for long anywhere. Kennedy was always away or on a job that kept him busy twelve to sixteen hours a day.

He had no hobbies, belonged to no clubs or lodges. He enjoyed three sports — golf, riding and swimming. He spent as much time with his family as he could without interrupting or delaying the work in hand. A result was that the brunt of caring for the schooling, training and direction of the children always fell upon Mrs. Kennedy.

Kennedy returned to New York to re-establish himself in private business, but he hardly had his hand in before the President called him back as fiscal adviser in the Foreign Aid Lend-Lease program. He sat with the President and the group of men Roosevelt had designated to supervise the expenditure of four billion dollars made available for it. In this position he became even more prominent in the news than he had been as chairman of the SEC.

When that project was organized and functioning, he resigned and again returned to New York to pick up the reins where he had dropped them, but this, too, was interrupted. Roosevelt called him to Washington to serve now as chairman of the Maritime Commission; his mission, to restore the American flag to the position it once held on the seven seas. In view of his experience during World War I, the President thought he was well qualified for the job.

⤳ 5 ⤵

THE NINE KENNEDY CHILDREN, at that time, graded off in height like steps. While Joe was reorganizing the Maritime Commission, Joe Junior was at Harvard. He had attended Dexter School in Brookline and prepared for college at Choate School. He resembled his father in appearance, had a ready grin and a pleasing personality, and made friends easily.

He had played end on an undefeated Choate football team; was vice-president of the Saint Andrews Society, editor of the yearbook, and won the Harvard football trophy awarded annually to the student who best combines scholarship and sportsmanship. From Choate, he went to London to study under Professor Harold J. Laski before entering Harvard. He intended to make a career of government, and presumably hoped to surpass his two grandfathers. Laski was the universally known Fabian socialist, chairman of the executive committee of the society, prominent in the Labor Party in England, author of a number of books

57

and works critical of capitalistic democracy. He had lectured at McGill, Amherst, Yale and Harvard.

Joe Sr. did not object. He approved. He felt that in a changing world his sons should be exposed, while they were still young, to different political concepts and philosophies, and thus be better equipped to meet a future in which they must play a part.

Wherever young Joe Kennedy went, Jack, only two years his junior, was not far behind. He was close enough in age to compete with him. Jack followed Joe to the London School of Economics, also studied under Laski, and then went on to Harvard. The two brothers were very much alike in looks, actions, tastes and interests, and they were close friends, although they did not always agree.

Because his father was away so much, Joe functioned as assistant father as well as big brother to the children. When young Joe was away, Jack took over and handled them just as effectively. If one brother did a thing exceptionally well, the other tried to do it better. Jack, too, was a good athlete and made friends as easily as Joe. Joe graduated from Harvard with honors; so did Jack.

Both were intense, impulsive and aggressive, always in competition; it was a curious brotherly relationship that was always good-natured, a succession of tilts indoors and outdoors in which each gave everything he had, win, lose or draw until the decision was established beyond all doubt, when it became immediately unimportant and was promptly forgotten. They were chums with complete understanding. In a pinch, one would drop everything to go to the aid of the other.

Joe broke his arm and his nose playing football at Harvard. Two years later, in the same sport, Jack suffered a back injury that was to plague him for years. Joe was dumped off a bobsled in Switzerland. He was patched up and returned to it. Either finished any sport covered with bruises. They kept in mind the family axiom — second best is a loser.

There were some differences however. Joe was quick-tempered; Jack's boiling point was much lower. Joe once leaped out of a chair in a Harvard dormitory to swing at a student who made a snide reference to John F. Fitzgerald, not knowing that Kennedy was his grandson. Joe's heart more often ruled his head. Jack was inclined to look at any problem from all angles; to study a situation, consider it carefully and contemplate his actions.

Jack did the same things Joe did, not because Joe led the way or pointed the path, but because their tastes in most things were almost identical. If Joe had lived, the probability is that he too would have been in politics and government although he and his brother might have been far apart politically. Joe's snap judgments and rigid adherence to a commitment or a position once taken, even when circumstances made it untenable, would have confined him to a groove, whereas Jack would not commit himself nor assume a position until he was sure, and even then he would give himself leeway to compromise or modify his position to meet changing circumstances.

Joe might have been the better baseball and football player, but Jack was the better swimmer and golfer. Both were good reporters for newspapers and for their father when he became Ambassador to England. Joe was good at reporting action at the scene, but Jack was by far the better writer, a researcher who could explain clearly what caused the action at the scene.

As a Hearst journalist, Jack did a high-grade, professional job. He had already written his book *Why England Slept* while he was still in college. Both had been close observers while in London with their father. Both had some understanding of British opinion and reaction, but Jack could define it and communicate it to others. The book became a best-seller. Jack had already achieved a reputation as a writer whereas Joe was only beginning to achieve one in politics in Massachusetts.

While Joe and Jack were at Harvard, Robert was too far behind them to be in competition — ten years old and in grade school — and Edward (Teddy) was still in kindergarten. The five girls were in schools. Rosemary, the eldest, had graduated from Sacred Heart Academy.

In large Irish families, it is a commonplace that at least one child shall have a "vocation," a divine call to the priesthood, the Christian Brothers or a women's religious order. All of the Kennedy children loved rough and tumble sports except Rosemary. She cringed and shuddered at violence of any kind; she was a spectator, but never a participant. Unlike her siblings, she shunned the limelight and was shy and retiring. It was inevitable, perhaps, that she should study at the Merrymount Convent in Tarrytown, New York, and devote her life to the sick and afflicted and particularly to backward and handicapped children.

She is the least publicized of all of the Kennedys. She

prefers it that way and her wishes are respected. An individualist who insists upon living her life as she sees it, she has smoothed the path for many a backward child. In this she has always had the complete support of her mother. In the distribution of the Kennedy charitable funds, both she and her mother have channeled hundreds of thousands of dollars to that end. She has always felt that too much public attention would destroy her effectiveness.

The Kennedys were gathered together as a family group usually during summer, Christmas and Easter vacations. Throughout the rest of the year they were scattered in schools or colleges. There were occasional weekends or holidays when all were accounted for in the same place, either at Hyannisport or Palm Beach. Wherever they were, they were in touch with father and mother by long-distance telephone every day. Headquarters and clearinghouse for all Kennedys then was the forty-sixth floor of the Rockefeller Plaza in New York where, if father or mother could not otherwise be reached, the calls from the children could be handled or rerouted.

In December, 1937, President Roosevelt asked Kennedy to accept the post of United States Ambassador to the Court of St. James. This caused a good deal of consternation among the Boston Irish. They could not decide whether to be flattered or indignant. In the heyday of P. J. Kennedy and John F. Fitzgerald, the Irish had the votes and the Brahmins the money. It appeared now that a time had come when the Irish had both the votes and the money. Old-timers wondered what Kennedy might do for Ireland, if anything, and wondered whether he had sold out to John Bull. Their sons and grandsons were not at all concerned.

Kennedy was not hesitant. He was stepping into a position of great honor, in which former Presidents James Monroe and John Quincy Adams had served before him; a post that had been filled by such men as John Jay, Edward Everett, Charles Francis Adams and James Russell Lowell. He went to London shortly after Christmas and found himself in the world's hottest corner.

It did not take Kennedy long to assess the situation. He decided that a good ambassador must be a good reporter. His chief function was to ascertain the facts and relay them to Washington. He needed trustworthy legmen, roving correspondents with sharp eyes and ears, and he had two such in his sons, Joe and Jack. Joe Junior finished his course at Harvard in three and a half years and joined his father in London a few months later; Jack followed when the summer vacation began. Diplomatic investigation became part of the education of each. They roamed the continent. Joe went to Spain to observe the Civil War there; Jack went east into Germany and Russia.

Joe and Jack were given their assignments by their father. Each completed his mission no matter where it took him. As a result of a tip that Joe Senior received, Joe Junior went to Spain to pick up a Communist spy named Cadesius. He persuaded him to come to London, made the necessary arrangements and brought him to the Embassy. The information he revealed was dispatched to Washington in the diplomatic pouch.

In the beginning, Kennedy's service in London created school problems. Mrs. Kennedy, Kathleen, Patricia, Robert and Edward were there. The girls were transferred from the Sacred Heart Convent in Noroton, Connecticut, to a convent of the same name in Roehampton, England. Robert and Edward continued their education in an English day school so that they might be home at the Embassy at night. Joseph Junior then became his father's secretary and Jack returned to Harvard. Jack, too, got his degree in three and a half years. All of the Kennedys were never assembled at the same time in London, but during the following summer they were reunited in southern France for a short vacation.

The Court of St. James probably never had a more outspoken ambassador than Kennedy. He presented Mrs. Kennedy and his daughters to the King and Queen because he felt that it was expected of him, and then closed the doors to all American women social climbers who came to London for that purpose because, as he explained, he disagreed with his predecessors. "I consider the practice of selecting each year a small number of young ladies from a long list, very few of whom the Ambassador has ever seen, to be presented at court as inequitable. Each year the Ambassador has been faced with this distasteful job of selection. It is undemocratic in that the invidious choice can have in large part no basis other than the pressure of recommendations behind the individual applicants, or pure chance. A large number of equally worthy ladies are disappointed and feel that they have been unfairly treated. It is impossible to choose properly from among them."

He confined presentations, therefore, to the families of American officials serving in England and to American families who were domiciled there. London newspapers characterized it as a bitter blow to the American big city social sets.

He made one other departure from custom that brought grins to the faces of the Boston Irish. He refused to wear the official knee breeches of the office, and appeared at the opening of the royal court season in evening clothes, long trousers, a tailcoat and white tie. Other Embassy officials, however, followed the custom and wore the regulation dress, and Kennedy permitted it.

Many of his statements stirred up criticism either in the United States or England or both. He was the first ambassador ever to speak at the Trafalgar Day dinner of the Navy League — an annual tribute to Lord Nelson — in which he expounded the theory he held then that it was unproductive for both democratic and dictator nations to widen the division existing between them by emphasizing self-apparent differences.

"Instead of hammering away at what are regarded as irreconcilables," he said, "they could advantageously bend their energies toward solving their common problems by an attempt to reestablish good relations on a world basis. There is absolutely no sense, common or otherwise, in letting these differences grow into unrelenting antagonisms. After all, we have to live together in the same world, whether we like it or not."

A few days after his Trafalgar Day speech, Nazi Germany stepped up its persecution of the Jews. The two appeared to be unrelated, but Germany's action seemed to be a form of answer to Kennedy's speech.

"What do you think of that?" a London newspaperman asked Kennedy.

He shook his head. "I think it's the most terrible thing I ever heard of," he said, "and I'll probably lose my job for saying it." He had observed earlier that London was a difficult assignment for an American diplomat because "you have to make good by what you prevent from happening rather than by what you cause to happen."

Kennedy became the close friend of Prime Minister Neville Chamberlain and reservedly approved his efforts to keep the peace with Hitler. As the war approached, he was more often found at 10 Downing Street than at the Embassy. Partly because of his close association with Chamberlain, in his own country, where distance did not lend enchantment to the view, Kennedy was characterized as an isolationist and an appeaser.

He did not consider himself either an isolationist or an interventionist. As a new ambassador taking a close look at England while learning the ropes, he described himself often as a middle-of-the-roader. As he viewed it, this was the only position to take until events determined which side of the road was the best and safest for his country to take. He regarded himself primarily as a reporter of facts upon which the President and the State Department would make decisions and he had an extensive staff to assemble these facts.

The Embassy, to the Kennedys, was just another home, another household. They had lived in many of them in Boston, New York, Washington and elsewhere, but their strongest roots were in Hyannisport. Any other house was a place in which to live until they could get back to Cape Cod. They were attached to that. Otherwise they felt at home anywhere.

For parents and the older children, the world had shrunk. They took planes for any place where they had a mission, or a reason to go, as casually as the folks back home boarded streetcars or called a cab. The current household would be in touch with father or mother by long distance or transoceanic telephone for advice, instructions or any emergency. Wherever a member of the family was, he or she could get back within a matter of hours.

Early in September, 1938, for example, Mrs. Kennedy was in Paris "for clothes and all that," as Joe explained it. The three youngest children and Rosemary, the eldest daughter, were in Cannes. Kathleen, the second daughter, was on her way east from New York, momentarily due in London. Jack was on the *Bremen* on his way west, due in Boston Saturday to return to Harvard. Brother and sister would pass each other on ships in the night. The two Joseph Kennedys were in the Embassy where either might take off at a moment's notice.

Living in London during those years did something to all of the sons and daughters; it gave them an international point of view and influenced their thinking. It even did something to ten-year-old Edward, who would one day captain the Harvard baseball team.

The Kennedys had brought over an American school-teacher to serve as a governess. Edward came home from school one afternoon and said: "Can I hit Romney over the head?"

The governess looked at him wide-eyed. "Why?" she asked.

"Every day when I come to school," he explained, "Romney hits me in the stomach. Mother says I must be polite to everyone and I mustn't do anything that would reflect on us; so I can't hit him back because my father's the Ambassador."

The governess looked down at Teddy grimly. "The next time Romney hits you in the stomach," she instructed, "you punch him right on the nose."

Teddy must have followed her advice. He and Romney became buddies.

❧ 6 ❧

KENNEDY WAS REASONABLY OPTIMISTIC during the summer of 1938. He felt that diplomacy could succeed in maintaining the peace, or if not, that it could contain a war in Europe. It was his conviction that the war, if it came, should be Europe's war and the United States should have no part in it; but the attitudes of Hitler, Mussolini and Stalin after Munich changed his opinion.

In September he told President Roosevelt that although he considered the German crisis to be serious, and although it was causing a good many Europeans sleepless nights, he did not think there was any risk that bombers would be over England within the immediate future, but his confidence began to fail quickly after that. Two months later, during the Thanksgiving season, he told a thousand businessmen in convention in London that he was no longer quite so sure. The Sunday punch already had been established as a modern military tactic by Hitler, and Kennedy told the group of a conversation he had had with the President before he became Ambassador.

"I was sitting in the President's office one day and he said to me, 'Joe, you've been working pretty hard for a long time. Go over to London and take it easy for a while. You know, they have weekends over there that last from Thursday until Tuesday.' Now, the word weekend to me is synonymous with crisis. I can't remember a weekend recently that somebody hasn't said, 'Something's going to happen on Saturday or Sunday.' "

Long before that, Kennedy had said to Roosevelt: "I'll take any job you want me to and even work for nothing at it as long as it's interesting. I never want to be bored."

He had not been bored. Reviewing the recent past, he recalled that for fifteen days during September until the Munich accord, Europe had been on the brink of war. Chamberlain's diplomacy of desperation ultimately resulted in his agreement with Hitler on the partition of Czechoslovakia, plebiscites in the remaining areas of that country and international guarantees of what was left of it by Britain, Germany and France — the Anglo-French plan accepted by the government at Prague. The tom-toms of war were beginning to sound louder and closer.

Mussolini, who had been on the fence, declared for Hitler. An angry public opinion against appeasement was mounting in England, France and the United States. The British government warned Hitler that if he attempted an armed invasion, Britain, France and Russia would come to the aid of Czechoslovakia. Chamberlain appealed to Hitler in a worldwide radio broadcast to cease and desist in the cause of peace. Kennedy reported to the President and gave his recommendations, and Roosevelt addressed a plea of peace to Hitler, Beneš, Daladier and Chamberlain. This had an effect — it delayed the war. As Chamberlain was about to go before Parliament to give an accounting of his efforts to avert war — and at that moment he was ready to acknowledge failure — a messenger rushed into Commons with a note. It was Hitler's answer to Roosevelt's second appeal to him. He offered a twenty-four-hour postponement of orders to march into Czechoslovakia until he could meet with the Premiers of Britain, France and Italy in Munich. Chamberlain went with his umbrella. The war was delayed, but the die was cast. It was now obvious to most observers that war must ultimately come.

During the period of uneasy peace, domestic life and business as usual continued at the Embassy. All of the girls and Edward were there and Continental travel was limited although they went occasionally to France and Italy. Kathleen was presented to London society at a dinner and reception in the English Speaking Union at Dartmouth House in 1938. Kathleen was pretty and witty, with a flair for writing that later made her a good newspaper reporter. She was popular, known to her family and friends by the nickname "Kick."

She met William Cavendish, Marquess of Hartington, eldest son of the Duke of Devonshire. He was young and handsome and had an eye for a pretty face and figure, but she was not immediately impressed by him. She met him again at a garden party attended by Princess Elizabeth. Kathleen got around a good deal, and was well liked among the debutantes in London. A London reporter described her as "gay, clever and unaffected." A French reporter who met all of the Kennedy girls en masse wrote: "Pat's the prettiest; Eunice is the most career-minded, but Kathleen is the one that everybody remembers." He insisted that the fact that she spoke French fluently did not influence his judgment.

A Boston society editor described her this way: "Her clothes were like her personality — attractive, not in the least showy, and completely suitable for whatever the circumstances in which she found herself. For tennis she would tie a big pink ribbon around her hair to match her pink piqué tennis dress. In the evening she wore demure and extremely becoming cottons and organdies in pale colors which set off her tan and her brown hair flecked with gold lights."

Hartington was being seen more often with her in London, at dances, the races and social events until their names were coupled and London society began to talk, but Kathleen, at nineteen, had no serious thoughts in her mind and the growing threat of war was giving London the jitters.

During the first eight months of 1939, as tension increased, life became both grim and exciting at the Embassy. Foresighted American nationals manning American business branches in England were abandoning the country. The Embassy workload increased. Hitler became even more arrogant. Washington needed neither Embassy eyes nor ears to discern what was going on or foretell the result. Hitler was determined to acquire the Polish corridor or a corridor to East Prussia at any cost and was screaming it in rabble-rousing speeches to his people. Diplomacy had become all but futile.

Jack Kennedy was then at Harvard finishing his courses, and Joe Junior had come back to Boston to wade into the political pool in preparation for the Democratic National Convention of 1940. Joe and Jack were residents of Boston and at twenty-one registered to vote. Legally it made no difference that Jack might live in a Harvard dormitory. He maintained an apartment in Bowdoin Square in the West End section of Boston, as did Joe. They were qualified to vote even though they might spend far more time away from their legal domiciles than in them. A traveling worker does not sacrifice his right to vote merely because he is away from home most of the time. This is a picayune charge sometimes made against Congressmen who spend very little of their free time, except during campaigns, in the districts they represent.

The Kennedy name was so well known that it was a foregone conclusion young Joe would be elected as delegate. He hardly needed to campaign. This would not be his first convention. He had attended others as a student at Harvard.

Although the result was certain, he canvassed the district, ringing doorbells, calling on voters, talking to Democratic leaders, working as hard as an unknown likely to be defeated.

He was elected handily. This was the third-term, precedent-breaking convention, and Joseph Kennedy, Jr., was unalterably opposed to a third term. Whether he discussed it with his father has never been revealed. James A. Farley and Joe Junior were good friends as were Farley and the senior Kennedy. Farley was so opposed to a third term that he resigned as Franklin D. Roosevelt's campaign manager. Farley's name had been mentioned as a possible nominee. Young Joe pledged his vote to him.

The convention machinery in Chicago had been well oiled and greased to nominate Roosevelt on the first ballot. When the roll was called, Roosevelt had 946 votes. Only 551 were required to nominate. The Massachusetts delegation gave Farley 12½ votes. A motion was made to make it unanimous, but when the Massachusetts delegation was polled, there was one stubborn vote for Farley — young Joe Kennedy's.

Delegates and leaders pleaded with him to change it. He refused. One of the Roosevelt leaders called Joe Kennedy in London and asked him to persuade his son to change his vote and make it unanimous.

"No," the Ambassador answered. "I wouldn't think of telling him what to do. He thinks he would be going back on his word."

The nomination of Roosevelt may have been ruled unanimous at that convention, but that lone vote in the Massachusetts delegation still disputes it.

The war in Europe began on Friday, September 1, 1939, when Germany attacked Poland without a formal declaration of war. Hitler proclaimed to the German armies that the Polish government had refused all offers of peace, persisted in persecuting Germans and had violated the frontier. He said: "No other means is left to me but to meet force with force." An hour later Polish cities were bombed by German planes. Poland called immediately for help from her allies, Britain and France. Commons was called to meet and to hear Prime Minister Chamberlain denounce Hitler for his senseless ambitions, the Nazi government and its methods of diplomacy.

All of this was hardly unexpected. London was already being evacuated. For days the American Embassy had been functioning in high gear, handling passports, visas, speeding American nationals on their way. Ships from Liverpool and Le Havre were overcrowded. The Embassy staff had been working from early morning until late at night.

Now the day had arrived.

France was rushing through plans for the evacuation of Paris. Declarations of war with Germany by both countries were imminent. Lost and forgotten Americans were turning up at embassies in London and Paris, anxious to get back to the United States. Two days later the four countries were at war. From that time on, all diplomatic action was on the neutrality front. Congress was called into session to pass the Neutrality Act of 1939. Italy, an Axis partner of Germany, declared its neutrality, and later reorganized its cabinet and replaced some members known to be pro-Nazi.

Joseph P. Kennedy had become unwelcome and unpopular in London. His views were too well known. He came back to the United States in December, when the pressure in the Embassy had eased up somewhat, to make his report to the President and stopped off in Boston long enough to say: "There is no place in this fight for us. As you love America, don't let anything that comes out of any country in the world make you believe you can make the situation one whit better by getting into this war."

"There is no reason," he went on in an interview reported in the *Boston Globe*, "no reason whatsoever, economic, financial or social, to justify the United States entering this war. One of the chief influences that might bring about such an involvement is the American people's sporting spirit in not wanting to see an unfair or immoral thing done, but let me repeat: This is not our fight. All of us want peace, but all of us have our own ideas of what peace should be. Under such circumstances who can say when there will be peace?

"If anybody advocates our entering this war, the American public should demand a specific answer to the question: Why?"

With such an attitude of mind, how could he be popular with Britons? They were already yearning and praying for us to get into it. He was frank, open, honest and outspoken in his opposition.

On the day that England declared war, Joe Kennedy's youngest daughter and son, Jean and Teddy, were in Ireland, out of harm's reach, although it had not been planned that way for the purpose. Kennedy had visited Ireland to attend a state banquet in his honor in Dublin Castle soon after arriving in England. He and Joe Junior had gone there to meet Eamon De Valera and Lord Mayor Byrne, obviously to discuss partition, although as Ambassador he would not reveal it and had nothing to say after their interview. It was his first visit to the birthplace of his four grandparents and he had made an occasion of it.

He and young Joe visited the ancestral homes of the Kennedys in Wexford Field in Cork and the Hickeys in Clonakilty. The two children remained there for a holiday. It was hardly a time to bring them back to London.

Joe and Jack were in Boston. That left Rosemary, Kathleen, Robert, Eunice and Patricia in London. Rosemary elected to stay, regardless of what might happen. Interested in the care of backward children, she wanted to complete a course she was taking. Her parents agreed. She remained in England until the following May and then went by plane from London to Portugal and then on to New York. Kennedy had been advising all American nationals whose presence was not required or essential to leave the country and placed the facilities of the Embassy at their disposal to expedite their departure. The presence of his own family certainly was neither required nor essential. As a husband and father, he had a duty to protect them.

It was anticipated that the Luftwaffe would come over and bomb London, and pilots and bombardiers would scarcely be concerned with the lives, buildings or properties of neutrals and their nationals. The Embassy itself and the house at Prince's Gate, where the Kennedys lived, were exposed, vulnerable and, according to recent experience with Hitler's war techniques, could conceivably be targets.

Mr. and Mrs. Kennedy decided that it would be wise to assemble the family once again in the United States — to return to the empty house in Bronxville. Joe, of course, would remain at the Embassy to carry on there with his staff and continue to maintain the house at Prince's Gate with the domestic staff there. The Kennedys arrived in New York in October, 1939.

Joe Junior and Jack were now immersed in national politics; Joe actively, Jack passively. In line with the family never-be-idle tradition, Kathleen spent the next three years working on the Washington *Times-Herald*. She became as popular there as she had been in London. The rest of the children were still in schools.

The war was static as far as England itself was concerned during the earlier part of 1940; the Luftwaffe did not come over her cities. The German armies were occupied elsewhere, while France was hiding behind the Maginot Line. The war spread out around the world from January until August; it touched some part of every continent, but England was temporarily spared its horrors.

The fighting centered in Africa where there were bombings; a naval engagement off Dakar in French West Africa. Arabs were killed in a raid on Aden, the British protectorate across from Eritrea. South America was at war only through the Guianas, Dutch, British and French; but the continent saw war when British warships chased the *Graf Spee* into the harbor of Montevideo, Uruguay, after a running fight along the coast.

Germany absorbed Austria and Czechoslovakia in 1938 and 1939. Albania had lost its independence to Italy. Finland surrendered a large slice of its territory to Russia. The

Soviet Union would destroy the independence of Estonia, Latvia and Lithuania and reach into Rumania and the Balkans. Kennedy watched all this transpire, coming home every three or four months to make his reports personally to the President. Through it all he remained adamant in his conviction that this was not America's war and that the country should stay out of it.

Early in April the Nazis invaded Denmark and Norway. The Low Countries would be next. Great Britain and France had tried to prepare for that by moving large forces into the Netherlands and Belgium. They were not enough — too little and too late. The Germans had superior air power, mechanized units, tremendous drive and surprise tactics.

The invasion of the Low Countries began on May 10. It was hopeless, a blitzkrieg driving the British and French troops to the sea. On that day the Chamberlain government fell. Winston Churchill replaced him as Prime Minister and gave his famous "blood, toil, sweat and tears" speech. King Leopold capitulated eighteen days later. Two days after that the British army was driven into the sea at Dunkirk, and Churchill said: "We will fight them from the rooftops. We will fight them in the streets." But the battle of France had now been lost. The Germans crossed the Seine, went on to Paris, flanking the Maginot Line on the way.

Joseph P. Kennedy, who would work at any interesting job because he hated to be bored, faced a grim prospect. What could diplomacy accomplish now?

The Battle of Britain began in August, 1940, when waves

of planes swept over the island bombing the naval centers along the Thames estuary. The Ambassador was in the same position, the same danger as any Englishman. He had no greater protection and in an emergency no more privileges. This is one phase of his service in England that he never has discussed. How he felt, what he thought during the raids, what he did when the walls of his house trembled and lamp shades fell across his bed while at the same time he was all but deafened by a nearby explosion — these considerations were always dismissed with a wrinkling of the nose and a wave of the hand when reporters asked him about them during his visits home.

The most he would say then was: "When you get as close to it as I am; if you could see what the bombs have done to London and to those who have to remain there, you would understand why I say this is not our war. In comparison with all of the strange and stupendous happenings in Europe recently, my experiences are insignificant."

When war was imminent, he advocated aid to England, but not intervention.

He demonstrated that he had physical as well as moral courage. German planes came over London day and night, sometimes attacking in mass raids of a thousand or more. Those who had to stay in London had no peace by day and little sleep at night. Kennedy's report to Washington was always statistical, never personal. His close calls and narrow escapes were reported by observers, London bobbies and newspapermen.

In the fall of 1940 several cottages were destroyed on an estate near his country house. On another occasion a bomb fell three hundred yards from it and a Nazi plane shot down by the RAF barely missed the place as it fell. His garage, in which some of his household lived, was bombed twice. In a daylight raid a bomb blew the car in which he was riding up on the sidewalk.

All told he was in two hundred and forty-four raids and during his entire term of service he was in a bomb shelter only twice; first, to inspect one in the Embassy and again when he was in Parliament listening to a speech by Winston Churchill when Nazi planes came over and everyone in the building was herded to the shelter.

When the Luftwaffe dropped a shell in his back yard with the inset initials "J.P.K." the Ambassador decided that the Germans meant to put him out of business.

Throughout this hectic period, Kathleen showed her unconcern by asking her father to release her from her pledge not to drink alcoholic beverages because, as she explained, "I'm always being invited around to houses for weekends. Fuel is rationed. They can't heat them and they're not warm. I'd like to take a glass of sherry just as other guests do."

Kennedy shook his head. "It would be a lot more practical and effective," he told her, "if you'd put on an extra sweater."

Early in November, 1940, Kennedy arranged to return to the United States to make an interim report to the President. He was not very popular in London at the moment, while at the same time his critics in the United States were calling attention to the association of the Kennedy family with Lady Astor and the Cliveden set. As an Ambassador, his popularity or unpopularity was always governed by his most recent statement. In any case, Londoners always knew where Kennedy stood even when he disagreed with them. He was forthright and never secretive.

When he left to return home, London newspapers were praising him "for the extreme cordiality reached in Anglo-American relations," to quote one of them. Before he returned almost all newspapers throughout the country would about-face and he would become one of the most unpopular persons in the kingdom.

Meeting Kennedy on these return trips was a standard assignment, usually handled by the same reporters. This time the *Boston Globe* sent Louis M. Lyons, a change from usual procedure. Lyons was a competent, careful and perceptive reporter. A graduate of Massachusetts Agricultural College, he had taught there for a while and then joined the staff of the *Springfield Republican*, where some of his stories attracted wide attention.

He joined the staff of the *Boston Globe* in February, 1919, and before long was covering top assignments. He covered the accession of Calvin Coolidge to the Presidency at the lamplit ceremony in the farmhouse in Plymouth, Vermont, after the death of Warren Harding, the return of Lindbergh after his 1927 transatlantic flight, and did an outstanding job of reporting the Lindbergh kidnaping trial.

He was one of the first nine applicants chosen for a Nieman Fellowship at Harvard and at the moment was doubling in brass as a *Globe* reporter and Curator of the Nieman Foundation.

Lyons brought along a Nieman Fellow companion, Ralph Colgan, an editorial writer with the *St. Louis Post-Dispatch*, to share the interview with him, but under the rules of the Fellowship, Colgan could not report it. He was present to obtain background only.

ৰঙ 7 ৰু

JOSEPH P. KENNEDY'S USEFULNESS as Ambassador to the Court of St. James ended that Sunday morning on which clicking teletypes also reported the death of Neville Chamberlain.

Because words were imprisoned in quotation marks and could not be pardoned, Kennedy stepped down from the world stage into the audience, an actor turned spectator, not sadder, but wiser. The ropes had been cut and the curtain fell with a crash that echoed in every world capital. The show ended suddenly in the very city in which Kennedy's career began.

Joe Kennedy did not see in advance the story that destroyed his influence as a diplomat. An exclusive interview had been arranged for Lyons and Colgan. It was not an "officially authorized" interview. He did not know what had been written about him until it was read to him that Sunday morning by a reporter filling in as Sunday city editor who had called him for another purpose. The reporter knew that Kennedy had been friendly with Chamberlain and asked him for a tribute. Kennedy was in Bronxville and the reporter in Boston. Kennedy was impatient. He said that Mrs. Kennedy was waiting for him to take her to church, and that he would prepare a tribute and suggested that the reporter call back. "That's quite an interview you gave Louis Lyons for this morning's paper," the reporter said.

"Why? What did he say?" Joe asked.

"What did he say?" the reporter repeated. "He wrote everything you told him. I've got it here: 'The Queen is one of the most intelligent women you ever met. It will be the Queen who will save what's left of England and not any of the politicians. . . . She's got more brains than the cabinet . . . Democracy is finished in England. The country will go Socialist . . . You'll spend everything you've got to keep us out of the war. If the United States gets into it with England, we'll be left holding the bag. . . . You're going to see Hearst about a campaign to keep us out of the war. . . . Our congressmen are dopes who don't understand the war or our relationship to it. . . . The only reason why the English haven't taken over Irish ports is because of American public opinion.' "

There was a dead silence on the other end. The reporter thought they had been cut off. "Do you want me to keep going?" he asked.

"He wrote all that?" Kennedy asked incredulously.

"All that and a lot more," he was told. "Anything wrong with it? You said it, didn't you?"

There was a pause on the other end. "I said it," he agreed. "I want you to read the whole thing to me, but not now. Rose and I have got to go to Mass. I'll be back in an hour. Call me."

The reporter could not get back to him in an hour. The London *Daily Mail*, the London *News Chronicle*, Reuter's, Amsterdam were calling by transatlantic phone requesting that full text be cabled immediately. It was nine o'clock in Boston; two o'clock in London. New York newspapers, AP, UP, INS were calling for confirmation and asking questions.

The Bronxville line was busy for hours. The reporter had to file his request with the operator and await his turn to get through. Then he tied the line up for half an hour. He read into the transmitter three full columns beginning with Lyons's description of Kennedy sitting in his shirt-sleeves eating apple pie and American cheese in his room at the Ritz-Carlton, his suspenders around his hips, and went on with:

"It was the setting for an interview that every American reporter has known 1000 times in visiting the head of the Elks, or the Rotarians, or the Lions Clubs — as American as apple pie."

Midway in his story Lyons quoted *St. Louis Post-Dispatch* editorial writer Ralph Coglan as saying: "I wouldn't be in your shoes. How do you know what you can write? He just puts it up to you to follow your own conscience and judgment and protect him in his diplomatic capacity. The last time I interviewed him in 1936, he poured himself out just like this, without laying any restriction on me, and I wrote every bit of it, and it went all over the country — the interview in which he said why he was for Roosevelt; and he said it was the best interview he'd ever had, but he wasn't Ambassador then. It all depends upon how you handle it. Any story can be told if it's told right."

When the reporter had completed the reading, Kennedy said, "He didn't miss a thing. He has destroyed me as an Ambassador. There is nothing left for me now but to resign."

"Why did you say it, Joe?" the reporter asked.

"I understood that I was merely giving them background and that it was all off the record," he answered. "He even quotes me in the last line as saying 'Well, I'm afraid you didn't get much of a story.'"

This left the reporter, acting as city editor, on a spot. He had called the managing editor during the break in reading the article and told him that Kennedy had confirmed the quotes, and all wire services and newspapers inquiring had been so notified. The managing editor got the impression that the story was now cleared.

Kennedy went to Washington the next day, publicly disavowed some of the statements in the interview, and saw the President. What he said to the President or what Roosevelt said to him, neither revealed, but Kennedy knew when he left the White House that he was through and could never again return to an intimate White House circle.

Nevertheless, he went the full distance for Roosevelt. On the following Tuesday night before election, he stepped before a microphone to present an address, sponsored by himself, his wife and the nine Kennedy children, to urge the election of Roosevelt on 114 stations of the Columbia network. He said he did it because he felt it was the best thing he could do for his country.

He resigned his post as Ambassador. The President did not immediately accept his resignation, but there was no doubt that he would. Kennedy returned to London to put his affairs in order. He was not exactly *persona grata* there. He made no apologies — there was no need for them. Now the world knew what he thought and he no longer could be effective in a diplomatic post.

Soon after publication of the story, Louis Lyons resigned from the *Globe* to become the full-time Curator of the Nieman Foundation at Harvard. There was no connection between this and the Kennedy story in the *Globe*. Arrangements to take it over had been made weeks before he wrote the story. He turned out to be an able Curator and the foundation has become of some importance in its announced purpose of elevating American journalism. A number of its Fellows have made impressive reputations, and Lyons himself has since won the Peabody Award for his outstanding radio and television reporting.

Kennedy forthwith discarded the gag that diplomacy had clapped over his mouth. He no longer needed to be careful about his choice of words. Once again he was entitled to free speech and he made use of the privilege. He was back on the air coast to coast on January 18, 1941, to urge America to arm itself to stay out of the war. He summed up his position in the first ten seconds. "Shortly before I came home from London," he began, "I spoke over the radio for the re-election of President Roosevelt. I declared then that my sincere judgment was that we ought to stay out of the war — that we could stay out of the war. I urged that we give England all possible aid. I feel the same way about it today."

He took time out in the half-hour broadcast to say a word about newspapers and newspapermen. "The saddest feature of recent months," he said, "is the growth of intolerance. Honest men's motives are being attacked. Many Americans, including myself, have been subjected to deliberate smear campaigns merely because we differed from an articulate minority. A few ruthless and irresponsible Washington columnists have claimed for themselves the right to speak for the nation. The reputation of the American press for fairness is being compromised by these men."

He protested that he had told the truth while he was in London. "I never thought it was my function," he said, "to report pleasant stories that were not true. Everyone will agree that had I, as your Ambassador, reported to our Government anything but the truth, I would have been false to my trust. I would have betrayed my country."

As Ambassador, Joseph P. Kennedy had usually been tactful in conversation, reserved, reticent and even taciturn, careful and selective of those to whom he talked freely. Private Citizen Kennedy spoke his mind frankly, freely and persuasively; he became an evangelist, going around the country pleading in auditoriums, banquet halls, colleges, at business conventions or wherever he found attentive ears, first that the United States arm itself to the teeth and next that it keep out of Europe's war. His thesis was that the United States should not fight unless it was attacked. He

preached this at the Commencement exercises at Ogle-
thorpe University where he received an honorary degree
in May. He urged it before the Advertising Club of Boston. He discussed it publicly and privately, anywhere and
at any time he was called upon to speak.

On July 15, 1941, Joseph P. Kennedy, Jr., with eighty
other young men from various colleges and universities enlisted at the Naval Air Station in Squantum, a suburb of
Boston. He was then twenty-six years old and had been
about to enter his senior year in the Harvard Law School.
In appearance he resembled his father very closely at that
age. His papers were endorsed; he was processed; he was
rated as a seaman second class while undergoing his preliminary training. He was issued his uniform and equipment, given a rigid physical examination, assigned to bar-
racks of college dormitory type and began his training that
afternoon. He was a familiar figure then around Boston
during weekends. Since his return from London he had
been living with his grandfather, John F. Fitzgerald, on
Beacon Hill in a suite at the Bellevue Hotel next door to
the State House.

He was appointed an aviation cadet on October 15, and
the next day reported at the Naval Air Station in Jackson-
ville, Florida, for flight training. He was still there when
the Japanese attacked Pearl Harbor, and was commissioned
an ensign in April, 1942.

Joe Junior liked the Navy. Jack liked the Army. For the
first time in their lives, it seemed, they would not be in
direct competition. As the younger brother, Jack had al-

ways been under the handicap that there was a difference of two years in their ages. Their likes, dislikes and ambitions always had been almost identical, but Joe always set the mark, made the record, won the victory and the honors two years earlier than Jack. In the tradition of the family and the manner in which they were trained, Jack must equal or better what Joe had done.

Jack followed Joe through the same schools. Although Jack was not so ardent a student as Joe, he nevertheless equally maintained his marks and at Choate School was elected "the most likely to succeed." Jack was determined to end the direct competition and after finishing at Choate, with the same honors as Joe, he defied family tradition and enrolled at Princeton, but that was not to be. During the summer before he was due to enter that university, his father sent him around the world to help round out his education. He contracted jaundice in the Far East; it recurred just before the Christmas vacation and Jack had to leave Princeton and thereby lost a year. The next fall he entered Harvard — back in competition, not only with Joe, but with Joe's record there.

Brother Joe, a favorite with Grandfather Fitzgerald, favored politics as a career. He had discussed it with his father, who approved. That was a blow to Jack. He, too, had the same political blood, the same ambition, and he realized it was one he could not now achieve because Joe had got there first. There could not be room for two Kennedys in Massachusetts politics. He was resigned to becoming a spectator at political conventions and Joe's chief adviser. He made up his mind to become a newspaperman. Writing was one talent that Jack had in far greater abundance than Joe.

Jack did just as well in his studies at Harvard as Joe. He topped Joe by making both the golf and swimming teams as well as the junior varsity football squad. He was a better swimmer than Joe and practiced the sport assiduously. Any contest or challenge, whether between themselves or against another team or adversary, made either or both go to almost absurd extremes to win.

Jack was certain, for example, that he could make the Harvard team that would swim against Yale, but a few days before the time trials were to be held, he came down with grippe and was confined to Stillman Infirmary. He was scheduled to compete against Richard Tregaskis, later Hearst's tall, lanky South Pacific war correspondent.

Jack was afraid that the hospital diet would leave him too weak to win. His roommate was Torbert McDonald — later to be a Congressman and prominent in Massachusetts politics. He persuaded McDonald to smuggle in milk shakes and small steaks. On the day of the trials he went AWOL from the infirmary, dived into the cold waters of the pool in the Harvard Indoor Athletic Building and as a result of his excess zeal not only lost to Tregaskis, but was in poor health for the rest of the school year.

Jack knew that he never could make the Air Corps. He felt sure that an old back injury that he had suffered in football would disqualify him, and just as he had tried once not to follow Joe into Harvard, he preferred to make his way onward and upward now in the Army, but once again he was to be disappointed; the back injury disqualified him entirely.

It is bad enough for any one of the Kennedys to come in second, but unthinkable that one should not even be able to get into a contest. Rejection made him all the more determined to get into the fight — and he was reasonably sure then that the United States would be drawn into the war. He was not particularly attracted to military service, but he spent months doing corrective exercises under the supervision of physical instructors, getting himself in shape, and finally wound up in September with a commission — in the Navy.

He became an intelligence officer and was assigned to desk duty in Washington, but he knew the right people and it was not long before he had himself transferred to deck officer training and finally wound up in command of a PT boat. He chose the service deliberately to prove a point. It was the most rugged type of service a man with a bad back could undergo because of the severe and continuous jouncing the boat took from the waves.

The reason for this perhaps was rooted in the character of the Kennedys. All of them were encouraged by both parents to be rugged individualists, to think for themselves, to stand by their convictions and to be completely independent, to stand together as brothers and sisters but to hold to their opinions even against each other. "If a thing is worth doing, it's worth doing well," was their father's favorite axiom, an injunction that they heard often individually and en masse. He might better have phrased it: "If a thing is worth doing, it's worth doing better than anybody else in the world can do it." He did not preach perfection. He would settle for pre-eminence.

Kennedy Senior himself, as a boy and young man, had been under the shadow of a parochially famous father. As he grew to manhood, he was known as "Pat Kennedy's boy, Joe." He doubled the ante when he married Rose Fitzgerald and acquired an ever more famous father-in-law, a political showman, a difficult actor to follow on any stage. Joseph P. wanted to be himself, and succeeded so well that before his death the elder Kennedy was known as Joe Kennedy's father and John F. was introduced at public gatherings always with the additional identification "Joe Kennedy's father-in-law."

Joseph P. Kennedy, Jr., had the same urge to get out from under his father's fame. He was more like his father than Jack. He looked more like him, talked and acted more like him. The two Joes were gregarious, quick to smile and make friends. Each had a ready wit, although young Joe's gift for it was superior to his father's. Young Joe was full of banter and wisecracks in any group. He had a gift, like both of his grandfathers, of making anybody he met think that he was the greatest guy in the world — a talent that makes votes grow like mushrooms.

Jack's problem was to get out from under the shadows of both. Kennedy had no favorites among his children, but the fact that Joe Junior arrived first demanded that he must be given attention first because he must reach each plateau in his life first. Jack and Joe were not alike. They had the same standards, but different ideas and talents. Joe was the hail-fellow, the good mixer. Jack was reserved, even shy. Joe's technique in a contest was to come out swinging and knock his adversary out in the first round. Jack's approach was studied, cautious. He knew that he would win finally. There was no need for haste, which so often makes waste. He looked for the weak points in his opponent, identified and isolated them, and then let him have it at the right moment.

In a debate, Joe had the stage presence, the confidence, the attitude of knowledge and authority. A good show-man, he won the audience by his presentation and when he was aroused, he shouted down his opponent. Jack achieved the same result by identifying himself with the audience, as though reasoning aloud with them, and walked off the platform the victor. Joe's good nature, his smile, his appearance would impress his audiences favorably; what Jack said would stay with them.

When the two fought together in a common cause, the combination of techniques was devastating — just as it was years later when the whole family got together and used a wider and more impressive combination of techniques to elect Jack Senator from Massachusetts.

Jack found it more difficult to get out from under the shadows of father and elder son. Circumstances sometimes conspired against him as they did when he enrolled at Princeton and now again when he wanted to join the Army.

At least he had the comfort of knowing that he and Joe were in different branches of the same service and that the fortunes of war would decide who would top whom.

Joseph P. Kennedy, who played a part in World War I and a more important one in the events leading up to World War II, would be compelled to sit this one out as anxiously as any other father with two sons in the service.

⊰ 8 ⊱

ON A STARLESS NIGHT in August, 1943, Lieutenant John F. Kennedy, skipper of the PT 109, was at the wheel patrolling Blackett Strait in the mid-Solomons. The sea was quiet and silent; then he saw the bow lookout turn his binoculars slowly and point and the man in the forward machine-gun turret called softly, "Ship at two o'clock."

Kennedy saw the shape. The PT boat was running slowly to avoid forming a wake and making noise. He spun the wheel, but it was too late. A Japanese destroyer, making forty knots, was heading straight for him. There was no escape, hardly time or need for a cry of warning. The crew stood tense for a moment waiting and the destroyer's bow crashed amidships, cutting it in two. Kennedy found himself on his back, watching the destroyer pass through as the PT splintered and parted in two. He drew himself up into a ball, hands hugging legs, to avoid being crushed by the gunwale, and just as his half-ship was being sucked down under water, he took a deep breath.

The water closed over him. He looked up and saw the glow of burning gasoline. He surfaced in the fire, flailing his hands to keep water about him. He looked around; saw the forward compartment of the PT still floating, its water-tight compartments still intact. He reached its side, called: "Who's aboard?" and could identify the voices of three enlisted men and an officer.

The rest of the crew, floating in Mae Wests in the water, identified themselves. All were accounted for. Two needed help. Kennedy swam to them and towed them to the floating hulk. There was hardly room enough on the half-deck to accommodate all of them and the engineer was so badly hurt that he needed most of it to stretch out in. The crew spent the night crouched and crowded on the deck — waiting. The hulk was beginning to gurgle. It could not last long.

When daylight came, the skipper saw that they were surrounded by Japanese islands: Kolombangara, where ten thousand Japanese were quartered; Vella Lavella, with more of them; Gizo, a Japanese camp; a group of small islands to the southeast — and the hulk was sinking. All but one of his men could swim. McMahon, the engineer, had been horribly burned.

Kennedy pointed to one of the small islands and said: "I'll swim there." He pointed to a floating timber from the wreck, directed the men to tie their shoes to it along with a ship's lantern wrapped in a life jacket to keep it afloat. They would swim along with it.

McMahon was placed in a Mae West life jacket. Kennedy took one of its long straps in his teeth and towed Mc-

Mahon to the island. It took five hours to reach it. He had been in the water for fifteen and a half hours, for he had remained in the water beside the hulk to make room for McMahon to stretch out.

He was salt-water-logged. He had swallowed too much of it while towing McMahon; it had lapped through his teeth. He had more swimming yet to do. As a navigator familiar with these waters, he knew that American naval patrol boats had cut through Ferguson Passage within sight of a reef beyond the point they had reached. He wrapped the ship's lantern more securely in its kapok jacket, put a rubber life belt around his waist, hung a .38 around his neck on a lanyard and instructed his men: "If I find a boat, I'll flash the lantern twice. The password will be 'Roger,' the answer, 'Wilco.'" He waded into the water to swim to the reef.

It was dark when he reached it. He misjudged its contour. He cut his shins and ankles on sharp coral, rested, and then swam an hour away from it into Ferguson Passage to tread water and wait for the hum of a PT motor. It was a long, and as it turned out, hopeless chance — none came through. He swam back to the island beyond the reef, flashed his light and called "Roger." One of the men answered "Wilco." The men, dull and dazed by their ordeal, thought he had found a ship. They could not comprehend that the skipper, flashing the light, was in trouble. Instead of swimming toward the light to bring him ashore, they waited as he drifted by the island, unable to make it.

Kennedy could never recall clearly what had happened. He slept, floating in the water, felt as if he were crazy — in a trance. The current carried him around the island and the reef and he became conscious at daybreak, to find that he was back in Ferguson Passage. He could not immediately orient himself. He thought he must be out of his mind. Once again he started to swim back to the island and felt as if he were dreaming. He had a nagging thought that he had done this before. Was he still doing it the first time? Had he done it before?

This time he managed to crawl up the bank on the island, retching and vomiting. The men rushed to help him. He singled out the hazy figure of Seaman Ross. "To-night, you take the lantern and the gun," he said, "and do what I did." He fainted or lost consciousness. That night Ross made it, but he found no help either.

The men were thirsty. There was no water on the island, but there were coconut trees on an island nearby. Kennedy pulled himself together. They decided to swim to the coconut island. Once again Kennedy towed McMahon with the strap in his teeth for three miles. They made it, found coconuts on the ground, broke them open and drank the milk. It made Kennedy and McMahon sick. The others either refused it or sipped it. That night it rained and they lapped water from the leaves.

On the fourth day, Kennedy and Ross swam to the island of Nauru and crossed it painfully to the Ferguson Passage side where they were lucky. They found a box of Japanese candy and hardtack, a keg of water and a one-man canoe. That night Kennedy paddled the canoe around Ferguson Passage, but again no PT's came. In the morning he paddled back to the men and gave them rations of water and hardtack. He was returning again to Nauru when a wind came up and swamped the canoe. A group of natives appeared from nowhere, rescued him and brought him to shore. They demonstrated that they were friendly by showing him where a two-man canoe was hidden.

Kennedy picked up a coconut and scratched a message on it with his jackknife. "Eleven alive. Native knows position and reefs Nauru island. Kennedy." The natives understood and paddled away. That night Kennedy and Ross paddled out into Ferguson Passage together. A storm came up. The waves were six and eight feet high. The tropical rain was so heavy they could hardly see three feet. The canoe was overturned and they swam back to Nauru, to fall exhausted on the beach.

They fell asleep and were awakened by a native with a note. It was from a Lieutenant Wincote in His Majesty's Service in command of a New Zealand infantry patrol on New Georgia. It instructed the party to follow the native and informed them that the lieutenant had already been in communication with the American authorities at Rendova to make plans to collect Kennedy, Ross and the rest of the party.

Kennedy and Ross were placed in the bottom of a canoe, covered with sacking and palm fronds and were paddled to New Georgia. That night he and Ross had tea in Lieutenant Wincote's tent. Soon he was on the way home in such precarious condition that it was abundantly clear that the active war was now over for him.

⚓ 9 ⚓

KATHLEEN KENNEDY, barely twenty-three in the spring of 1944, was a very pretty girl. She found her job at the Washington *Times-Herald* interesting enough, but she decided that a time had come when she, too, should get into the war. She joined the Red Cross and because she was familiar with London, it was arranged that she would serve there. Perhaps there were other reasons. Kathleen liked London, and the Marquess of Hartington of the Coldstream Guards was there when he was on leave.

Within the family, Kathleen, as the next to eldest girl, was in the same relative position among the girls as Joe was among the boys. The girls looked up to her. Joe and Jack had gone; now she was going. They would miss her. Within a couple of weeks she was serving doughnuts and coffee to Allied soldiers in London's famous Hans Crescent Club. She was a favorite among American GI's, who still remember her as unaffected, friendly and a good sport, the words they used then to describe her. Once again she was seen going about with William Cavendish and all London knew now that it was serious. Their engagement was announced on May 4 and two days later they were married in the Chelsea Registry Office. The marriage surprised her friends in the United States, particularly in Boston, not because of the groom's rank, but because he was a non-Catholic. In characteristic Kennedy tradition, she had made her own decision. Another fillip of the wedding was that because of wartime restrictions on food, rice could not be thrown upon the couple; instead, they were showered with rose petals.

The Duke of Devonshire was on hand, as was Lieutenant Joseph P. Kennedy; they were the only members of the family who could make it between the announcement of the engagement and the marriage. A reception was held in London because the Viscountess's Devonshire house had been hit in a raid. Among the two hundred and twenty guests were Red Cross workers and GI's from the Hans Crescent Club who rubbed shoulders with the Duke of Devonshire and the Dowager Duchess, the Duke's sisters and Lady Astor, the Duke of Rutland and Lady Salisbury.

The marriage made Kathleen a member of one of Great Britain's wealthiest families. Her father-in-law maintained more establishments than any other peer. She was the second American to marry into the family. Adele Astaire, the dancer, was the first; she had married Lord Charles Cavendish.

Kennedy was out of the government and out of the war, but he was never out of the news. What he did, what he said, what he thought, was grist for columns and columnists. He was accused of being almost everything — a Fascist, a reactionary, an isolationist, a turncoat from Roosevelt supporter to Roosevelt hater. He came to Boston after Kathleen's wedding and was interviewed at the Ritz-Carlton Hotel.

"Joe," a friendly reporter said, "they say you're a Fascist."

"What's your definition of a Fascist?" he countered. "The word can mean anything today and is applied to almost anybody. If you mean by Fascist a person who believes in totalitarian government, it can't apply to me because I have dedicated the past several years of my life to perpetuating and protecting the democratic form of government. I don't have to defend myself against that. The charge means nothing. It is made loosely against almost anybody today.

"Who are they who say these things, and how do they get that way? They are said or written first by irresponsible columnists and commentators who pretend to have inside information. They dream up a set of circumstances that seem to justify a conclusion and present them. They can't name the informant because there is none and then the conscientious and reliable analysts and commentators call me for verification and the denial never catches up with the falsehood.

"Sometimes it is libelous and actionable, but not to such a degree that a victim feels compelled to do something about it. It is better judgment to ignore it than to make an issue of it and focus further public attention upon it.

"It is an unfair, unwarranted intrusion into the affairs

of any public figure who tries diligently to mind his own business. I don't think that I have ever been difficult to reach, and I have been reasonably frank both on and off the record. It is one thing to violate an off-the-record confidence either purposely or mistakenly, and quite another to assume a set of facts and present them as the hidden truth.

"It is true that I do not and have not always seen eye to eye with the President or with some of the other advisers who surround him. We have and have had differences of opinion, some of them diametrically opposed and deep-seated, but they were honest and true to their convictions and so was I. I have never leaked information concerning them to any member of the press, and I am quite sure that they would not, either. It would be beneath their dignity, and yet embarrassing rumors are widely circulated.

"Certainly it doesn't help the war effort to manufacture or originate such rumors. It gives aid and comfort to the enemy and becomes fodder for propaganda indicating that we are divided. It's comparable to treason."

He paused, thinking it over, smiled and then went on. "What I've been saying here could be tortured into language that might support the suggestion that I am a Fascist, that I favor censorship to keep such rumors away from the eyes and ears of the enemy — and yet I am as much opposed to such censorship as any writer, broadcaster or publicist; so perhaps you'd better keep it off the record for the time being."

Kennedy's reaction to this kind of journalism points up a common problem that confronts reporters, celebrities and public figures from time to time, as his sons John F. and Robert and his daughter Eunice would discover later when they became newspaper reporters and foreign correspondents. Newspaper men and women often get valid news and tips from responsible and unimpeachable sources and feel an ethical obligation to protect the informant, even though they might go to jail for contempt of court.

The celebrity or public political figure who engages press or public relations counsel is immediately suspect. The star of stage, screen, sports or any kindred medium has something to sell or to exploit. His, or her, objective is free time or space. The political figure, always a candidate or potential candidate, may have much the same purpose in mind, or he may have something to hide, in which case, his press agent is an expert in changing the subject.

It is true that there are columnists and commentators who can expand a chance remark or a fleeting thought and deck it with fancy embroidery until it becomes an impressive spread, but they are easy for the discerning reader to distinguish.

"Your critics also say that you're an isolationist," the reporter reminded Mr. Kennedy.

"Who says so?" He bristled. "And how can anybody make a charge like that stick? I have four children in the service — or at least I will have very soon — two sons, a daughter and another daughter soon to enlist. Jack is back in this country after having a motor torpedo boat shot out from under him. I never wanted this war. I don't think anybody in the United States wanted it. I opposed it with all the vigor I could command. I had a close-up of this war and all that it means long before the American people did. I was bombed in the Battle of Britain. A bomb with my initials on it fell in my back yard. I was in an automobile that was blown up on the sidewalk. I reported honestly to the President what I heard and saw and I urged that we keep out of this war.

"I am not an isolationist," he continued. "I never have been one. I was against our entry into this war until we were forced into it. Long before Pearl Harbor I favored all aid to England short of war, and I urged it. I favored buying time with war supplies — so that we could rearm — and events have justified my judgment. We bought time that way until Pearl Harbor; and we rearmed England to pay for our opportunity to retool, to draft an army and train welders and war workers. After Pearl Harbor there was no more time for sale. Unfortunately, I haven't been given an opportunity to do the kind of job I feel able to do in this war. My sons have had the opportunity and they're in."

"They say," the reporter went on, "that you favor monopolies; the same old system that held labor down and concentrated great wealth in the hands of a few. They say that you've cornered the market on Scotch whisky, that you're responsible for its shortage; that you're investing your money in real estate, buying race tracks, hotels, theater chains and railroad properties because real estate will neither inflate nor shrink."

"That," he answered, "is pure bunk. I bought 9000 of 52,000 shares in Hialeah Race Track from Colonel Bradley. Nine thousand shares is not a controlling interest.

I have bought no property in New York. In the name of my sons, three pieces of property in New York have been purchased for $400,000.

"Drew Pearson discovered that I owned shares in the RKO theater chain in New England. You've known that for years; so have Arthur Krock, Joe Timilty and so many of my friends that I can't even number them; but it was news to Drew Pearson. He rushed into print with the statement that I had bought a chain of theaters.

"That's typical of Pearson. If he had checked it, he would have discovered that I have owned the stock for twenty-two years. I haven't bought any railroad property and I haven't bought any hotels. As far as Scotch whisky is concerned, I have a four months' supply in warehouses — not a four year supply — and I never have had on hand anything larger than a four months' supply."

"They say you are building fences and making yourself politically powerful in Florida."

He bridled at this. "Who the hell would want to be politically powerful in Florida?" He glowered. "To what purpose and for what end would I want that? It's nonsense."

"They say you're in favor of a negotiated peace."

"Why not?" he answered. "That's what it will finally come to anyway. In the end we've got to negotiate with somebody. We'll negotiate before an armistice in order to achieve peace, and we'll negotiate after an armistice with whoever happens to be in power in Germany and Japan, and then my guess is we will finally find ourselves in a position where we will have to negotiate with Russia because I think that Russia will be the dominating force in Europe when this war ends.

"Winston Churchill has said that he was not made the King's minister to preside at the liquidation of the British Empire — but he will, or his successors will. Britain will lose India and the ties that bind Australia and Canada are no longer so tight.

"We were offered a chance to negotiate a peace with Germany nine months ago," he went on, "but neither Churchill nor Roosevelt would listen. Mme. Chiang Kai-shek came to the United States and had with her the peace terms offered by Japan. I'm probably one of three men in this country who knew what they were, but perhaps I'd better not continue with that for now. When this war is over, Russia will dominate the Balkans, eastern Germany, Italy and possibly the Mediterranean. If the Vatican ever comes within the Russian orbit, and that is a threatening possibility, it will pose a problem for every Catholic in the world.

"Assuming that we do make an agreeable deal with Russia, which I doubt, where are we? We will be in a world with two contradictory political philosophies and we will be confronted by two alternatives. Will Russia force Communism down the throats of European nations who do not want it? Will we force democracy down the throats of European nations who do not want it? Not all of these European nations are capable of self-government. Are we going to 'make' them democratic by force? Do we negotiate a peace with them and let them run their governments as they see fit and do business with them — or do the three big powers who come out of this war, the United States, Britain and Russia, conquer them and keep them in subjection?"

He had been characterized in newspapers and magazines as a reactionary, clinging desperately to old forms, modes and customs in a changing world. That did not seem to fit him. Reactionaries may have been glad to acknowledge him as one of their own, but they could not. He would not fulfill the definition. Liberals would not acknowledge him because of the fact that he conformed in so many ways. He was neither fish nor fowl; he was an imponderable in the American political scene. It had been printed that he was a Roosevelt-hater. He was taxed with that.

He shook his head. "I don't hate Roosevelt," he said. "I never said so. You can differ with a man and depart from him without hating him. I am not determined to defeat him for a fourth term. I may support him this year just as Al Smith will. I can't definitely say at this early date in May before the conventions and the campaigns. If I am convinced that his election will serve my country best, I'll support him. I am first, last and always an American, and these are not mere words falling from my lips. I mean them. My personal feelings are unimportant. I'm thinking of my country after this war.

"I helped to elect Roosevelt three times. I knew and approved of his social reforms when I did so. I played a leading part in putting at least one of them into effect. I have never opposed him. I found some fault with the way in which some of his subordinates interpreted the New Deal.

"I am not concerned with the threat to my world, but I am alarmed at the threat to our democratic form of government. My world may pass. It can't go on forever. The world must go forward. It can't go backward. The generation that follows me may have to stand for everything that I stood against — and I realize that includes even my own sons. I made my choice among the philosophies offered when I was young. Each of them will have to make his or her own choice.

"At the same time, I have no intention of turning my back on and abandoning the world that I knew. It has been a good world to me and I'll fight for it. There are systems of government that are designed to replace it. I want none of them. In my view of it, any one of them — Communism or dictatorship — would make a worse and not a better world. My world has its faults, but it brought me from the mudflats of East Boston to the Court of St. James. It brought me success and honors in business, government and the academic world — things that I never could have achieved under any of the systems of government that are offered as substitutes.

"Reforms may improve the Republic and its democratic form of government, but I'll fight to the last ditch against any attempt to change that form of government. That would be a long step backward, not forward. If the American people change their form of government themselves, that would be democratic and I would be disappointed and defeated; but they would be doing the changing and I would have no complaint even though I had done my best and spent whatever I had in trying to persuade them not to change; and I would accept it. I do, and always will, stand against any attempt to change that form of government in any other manner than by the people themselves with their ballots in the polling places. I never can stand by and see such a change impressed upon them by a minority; or put over on them while a million or more men and women are fighting to preserve the form of government that they knew. This war never can be an excuse for that kind of change."

"They say you're an appeaser?"

"They're wrong if they say that in the present tense," he answered. "I was an appeaser in an era when it was good policy. I favored buying time with appeasement when we were helpless and unarmed. Long after circumstances compelled me to abandon appeasement, it still was the policy of our government. I had nothing to do with the appeasement of Japan with scrap metal, oil and supplies almost up to Pearl Harbor. I certainly could have had nothing to do with the appeasement of Spain long after I returned to private life. Many of today's critics of appeasement of the past would do well to turn the light of criticism back upon themselves in the present. I considered it good policy to appease to buy time. Some people in public life today appear to think that it is still good policy to appease and buy nothing."

❧ IO ❧

UNTIL PEARL HARBOR, Joseph P. Kennedy, Jr.,
had the same convictions about war as his father. Less than
two years later he was rated as one of the best Liberator
pilots in U-Boat Alley flying daily missions over the Bay of
Biscay. He had completed his quota of missions and was
eligible to return home on leave when one of those chal-
lenges that would nag him forever if he did not accept it
came his way. "Project Anvil"— top secret — was revealed to him. He was immediately interested. He wanted
to be in on it; volunteered for it; refused his leave and persuaded his crew to remain for a special assignment.

Project Anvil was the precursor of the modern-day
pilotless plane navigated by remote radio control — a robot, developed jointly by the Army and Navy, that could
be directed to the target from a "mother" plane or dual
parent planes. Its specific purpose in World War II was to
destroy a special strategic target — the V-2 rocket-launch-
ing site in Normandy.

It had been given exhaustive tests in the United States.

The Navy's Special Air Unit 1, a part of Fleet Air Wing 7, of which Kennedy, Jr., was a member, was designated to make further tests in England and to carry out the mission for which it was designed. In the tests, carrying ten tons of mock explosives, it behaved precisely as it did in United States trials. The robot plane required a pilot to get it off the ground and into the air where the parent planes would take over. Pilot and co-pilot would parachute to the ground and be recovered.

Kennedy elected to take the robot plane off the ground. Lieutenant Wilford J. Willy of Fort Worth, Texas, volunteered to go along with him. D-day for them came on August 12, 1944. The robot, or drone — a Liberator — was laden with ten tons of high explosives when it was taken off the ground by Kennedy and Willy. The Liberator performed exactly as specified. The parent planes were Vega Venturas, twin-engine bombers, in which the controls had been installed. All of them had been tried, tested and approved at the Naval Air Station at Traverse City, Michigan. Special equipment had been installed at the Naval Air Materiel Center in Philadelphia and the planes had been ferried to England and had been secretly based at Winfarthing (Fersfield).

They had been guarded carefully. There appeared to have been no opportunity for sabotage. Army and Navy sentries had patrolled the hiding place twenty-four hours a day. A special radio search of air waves had been made to make sure the enemy was not using the frequencies on which the drone would be operated. Both accompanying planes had been checked out in perfect order. Either plane could operate the drone by remote control. One would take over if the other failed. Kennedy, in command, had been flying PB4Y's for more than a year. Willy had been in the Navy for sixteen years, three of them devoted entirely to radio control projects.

All three planes took off on schedule. Radio controls, according to ground checks, were correct. Soon after the takeoff at 6:20 in the evening, when the planes were approaching the English coast, the drone exploded in two blasts, a second apart. Kennedy and Willy were killed. The wrecks were examined minutely, but no cause for the explosions could be established. Neither pilot nor co-pilot could have been responsible. All switches and safety devices were found to be in order. The accompanying planes had not yet taken over and could not until the pilot and co-pilot bailed out. Nothing was found to have been wrong with the firing circuits. The only answers the experts could give were sabotage; an almost impossible hit from friendly flak; static electricity in the air; electric heating of a fuse from an unknown source; gas leakage ignited by an electric spark or an imponderable which no one could have conceived or foreseen.

The Army and the Navy were interested in the cause, the Kennedy family no less so; they were in mourning. In any case, Kennedy and Willy proved something at the cost of their lives. Because of them, a history-making Skymaster flight was made from Newfoundland to England a month later. A second drone was perfected, too late to destroy the Normandy rocket site. The Nazis had abandoned it, but Lieutenant Ralph Spaulding, USMCR, took a drone off the ground, bailed out, and the drone destroyed the Nazi submarine pens at Helgoland.

Kennedy's body never was recovered. He was officially declared dead and awarded the Navy Cross, the American Defense Medal, the European-African-Eastern Area Campaign medal. A destroyer, the U.S.S. *Joseph P. Kennedy, Jr.* was named in his honor. His brother Robert, who was later to make quite a name for himself as a Senate Committee inquisitor, was also to reject a commission in the Navy to serve as an able-bodied seaman on that destroyer during the Korean War.

Lieutenant Joseph P. Kennedy, Jr., and Lieutenant Wilford Willy, six years his senior, and father of three, had been close friends. They got along well and understood each other. They were far apart by birth and background. Willy was a career man in the Navy; he had enlisted in June, 1929, as an apprentice seaman, and the Navy had thereafter become his life. He took its courses in aviation and radio and became a noncommissioned pilot and expert radio technician. When the war came he was fit, ready, willing and able. He was commissioned a lieutenant (jg) in March, 1942, and became a lieutenant in June.

He and Joe had struck up a friendship; he was never overawed by the fact that Joe was the son of an ambassador. They were always together, kidding and roughhousing. Willy got the same decorations and commendations as Joe, and his wife received them as five hundred officers and men stood at attention at the Naval Air Station in Clinton,

Oklahoma, on March 21, 1945, a day that the Kennedys will never forget.

Joe Kennedy exerted an influence upon all of the Kennedys during his life and continues to do so even now long after his death. He is never out of their minds for long and his name will remain in the public mind long after the Kennedys have departed, particularly in Boston and New York where it identifies hospitals and charities built or financed by the Kennedy Foundation. His brother John F. memorialized him in *As We Remember Joe*, a collection of tributes and the reminiscences of teachers, instructors, brother officers and personal friends who knew him intimately.

The number of copies was limited and the book has since become a collector's item. Dedicated to his father and mother, it is also a tribute to the fathers and mothers of Billy and George, Cy and Gil, Chuck and Peter, Moe, Demi and Orv, the airmen who served with him and were killed in action.

The year 1944 was a bad one for the Kennedys. Less than a month after Joe was killed and four months after the marriage of Kathleen to the Marquess of Hartington, he was killed in action while leading an infantry charge of the Coldstream Guards in Normandy. When the news came, Kathleen was with her father and mother in New York, where she had come from London to be with them after the death of her brother. Joe had sacrificed his leave because of the challenge of a new and untried weapon of war; the Marquess had been in command of a unit because he had been defeated at the British polls.

Just before they were married, Hartington had decided to go into politics and stood for Parliament. He had waged a vigorous and intelligent campaign — lost, and returned to his regiment. Kathleen returned to England for her husband's funeral and decided to make her home there.

⊰ II ⊱

THE KENNEDY FAMILY emerged from the war badly hurt. Jack picked up the threads of Joe's life and set out to do all of the things that his brother would have done. It was a natural and proper choice in the eyes of all of the Kennedys. They knew that Joe would have approved. Joe would have been a candidate in the Democratic primary for election to Congress after the war. Jack took out nomination papers and announced himself as a candidate. Joe would have picked the Eleventh Congressional District. Jack did so for the same reason.

A Boston mayor has a four-year term. Out of office, James Michael Curley had parked himself in Congress from the Eleventh District. He did not live there. The law did not require it. He had a beautiful house on Jamaicaway far outside its boundary, but any Congressional district in the Boston Metropolitan area would vote for Curley if for no other reason than force of habit.

A city election was upcoming in 1946 and it was a foregone conclusion that Curley would move out of Congress and back into his familiar spot in City Hall. When he made public his intention, there was a free-for-all, a wild scramble among Boston politicians. Nine of them appeared, including John Fitzgerald Kennedy, described by the others as a good-looking, tousle-haired kid, still wet behind the ears, who didn't know his way around and was trading on the fact that he was the grandson of two well-known political leaders and the son of Joe the ex-Ambassador who had plenty of dough to finance a campaign.

This description of young John F., shouted through loud-speakers in city squares and from sound tracks touring the streets, from platforms in municipal buildings and public assembly halls, did John F. no good. He was target-for-tonight for eight ambitious men who knew, as everybody in Boston does, that nomination in the Eleventh District is tantamount to election. A Republican in the Boston segment of this district would get hardly enough votes to count.

The Eleventh Massachusetts District, however, is a contradictory and unpredictable place. It is made up of Wards 1, 2, 3, 22 in Boston; all of Cambridge; and Wards 1, 2 and 3 in Somerville. Boston Wards 1, 2 and 3 are East Boston, Charlestown, the North End and West End; 22 is Brighton.

Wards 1 and 3 of Boston are populated predominantly by Italians and Italian descendants with a scattering of Irish. They were the earlier strongholds of P. J. Kennedy and John F. Fitzgerald and the old-timers remembered them affectionately. Many fathers and mothers there would have been sure to tell their sons and daughters as they left their houses on primary morning: "Don't dare come in this door tonight if you voted for anybody but Jack Kennedy."

Ward 2, Charlestown, is unique. There is no community exactly like it anywhere in the world. It has a cohesive population, made up of sundry and diversified races, almost all Catholic. A person who lives there may speak his mind and disagree with the man next door or with a stranger at a bar, but if he is a stranger and does so he risks a trip by ambulance to City Hospital. For years the Health Department maintained a branch "Relief Station" in City Square for that among other purposes. A rule that outlanders learn quickly there is: "Never knock anybody; he may have a friend within earshot. Or better still, don't open your mouth except to order a drink." The people there are like those in Brooklyn, fiercely loyal to each other. Their fights are family affairs and would-be peacemakers had better remain silent while they are in progress. It is probable that there is not a single Republican anywhere in Charlestown.

The collective population is accident-prone and addicted to errors. Historically, it is steeped in mistakes. Paul Revere in song, poem and story, stood on its shore waiting to ride and spread the lantern alarm — one if by land, two if by sea — and this episode never happened that way, according to the research of Esther Forbes in *Paul Revere and the World He Lived In*. Actually, Paul was in the belfry of the Old North Church giving the signal to his confederates on the other side. Furthermore, a probability is that Paul, after he joined them, began his ride in Cambridge, not Charlestown.

Historically nothing about Charlestown ever has been

definite or established. The first battle of the Revolution was fought there (or was it?). It was called the Battle of Bunker Hill, where Major General Israel Putnam or Colonel William Prescott or General Joseph Warren gave the order: "Don't fire until you see the whites of their eyes." There has not only been continuing dispute about who said it, but also about whether it was an intelligent or stupid order.

In any case, years later the citizens of Charlestown persuaded the legislature to build a towering 450-foot monument on Bunker Hill and declare the day a city-wide holiday forever. When the monument was completed, Charlestonians discovered to their consternation and chagrin that it had been built upon the wrong hill. The battle, historians pointed out, was actually fought on Breed's Hill. Little could be done about it then and Charlestown political leaders dismissed it with the attitude: the hell with it — it's a nice monument.

As a holiday in perpetuity and so legally declared, it is observed only in Charlestown. The rest of the city ignores it entirely and conducts business as usual, but in Charlestown it becomes the justification for a wild bender that begins the night before with open house — and that means everybody's house in the district — and continues through packed Mardi Gras streets, a long afternoon parade and winds up throughout the next day with the world's largest collection of hangovers and big heads.

Charlestown is, perhaps, the only place in the world where a property owner would sell all of the land surrounding his house, watch a square of red brick buildings go up around it and then discover that he had neglected to retain an easement that would give him access to his house; and be compelled to tunnel through one of the newly erected buildings to acquire one. Misjudgments like that are commonplace there.

The district is like an attic and cellar to Boston, a handy place to put unsightly things that nobody wants, like the State Prison and the electric chair. Thousands of its people live in darkness under an elevated railway structure; more thousands live under the approaches to the high Mystic River Bridge and more in the shadow of overhead ramps and under the overhead freeway that bypasses the section from the North into Boston.

It has the Mystic River on one side, Boston Harbor on the other. The harbor shoreline is studded with grain elevators, oil tanks, piers and wharves. On a third side are acres of freight yards and on the fourth factories, including one that makes chemicals of a mountain of yellow sulphur in Charlestown's back yard. Thus the population is made up of longshoremen, dock wallopers, freight handlers and factory workers.

It still has some of the worst slums in the city, crying for urban redevelopment. When federal and city funds became available for the purpose, radio and television crews moved into the area to tell the story, but before the cameras and microphones could be set up, the crews were surrounded by an ominous and threatening mob, who demanded to know what they were there for, and all about it.

They then decided that they would have none of it; they liked the place as it was. A spokesman ordered the crews to pack up and get out and saw to it that they did. They were escorted to the Boston side of the Charles River bridge and ordered never to come back into the ward again.

This is part of the voting population Jack Kennedy proposed to represent. On the other side of the ward was another bridge across the Mystic River leading to Cambridge where Kennedy would be representing the professors, resident staffs and faculty members of Massachusetts Institute of Technology and Harvard University.

The third generation of Kennedys had now arisen to plague Curley. He did not relish the idea of a popular candidate representing the Eleventh District. He felt it belonged to him. He could occupy it whenever he felt like doing so. It was like a spare room in his political household, a place to retire with pay and to rest and recuperate whenever he was defeated or out of office.

When the list of candidates was complete, a reporter stopped by at Curley's house and showed it to him. "Who do you think will win?" the reporter asked.

Curley always answered such questions honestly. He looked over the list, squinted dolefully at the name John F. Kennedy and answered: "Kennedy! How can he lose? He's got a double-barreled name, John Fitzgerald Kennedy, named for two well-known officeholders. His grandparents will be remembered. He doesn't even need to campaign. He can go to Washington now and forget the primary and election."

The fact that this was so did not please Curley, but he was trapped as he so often had been by a Kennedy. As a candidate for Mayor, John F. Fitzgerald was supporting him. Pat Kennedy had died in 1929, and Curley could not now use his influence to defeat Kennedy.

During that primary campaign for Congress, Boston looked on pop-eyed at its first experience with the phenomenon of the one-for-all and all-for-one organized Kennedys: his mother, brothers and sisters who flew into Boston to work for Jack. They swarmed into the wards, going from house to house, ringing doorbells, persuading and canvassing for votes for Jack. They gave teas and parties, attended his rallies. They went into the slums, cradled babies, visited, sympathized and told thousands of voters what a wonderful brother Jack was.

Mother and daughters went through rough, tough and rugged individualist Charlestown like a swarm of bees. Word preceded them from house to house. Housewives swept and dusted, cleaned up, got ready and put on their best clothes to greet them. They drank tea and talked about the things that interest women in tenements and downstairs kitchens. The other candidates had never experienced anything like this.

It wasn't long before Charlestown men in bars, taps and on street corners were inquiring, "What are these guys knocking Jack Kennedy for? I remember John F. when he was Mayor." Or, "My father remembers him and old P.J. They were a couple of good Joes. Suppose this kid is young. He'll do as good for us, or maybe better than anybody else."

He won in a walkaway. His nine opponents were snowed under.

↞ 12 ↠

WHEN JOHN F. KENNEDY went to Washington as Congressman, his sister Eunice was already there. She, too, had come quite a distance in government within a few years. She had been attending Roehampton Convent of the Sacred Heart while her father was Ambassador. She returned with the family in 1939 to New York and enrolled in the Manhattanville College of the Sacred Heart. Later she transferred to Leland Stanford University in California where she majored in social studies and graduated in 1943.

She went to New York to do case work in Harlem for a year and was drawn into the Special War Problems Division of the State Department dealing with American prisoners of war in Germany. In January, 1947, Attorney General Clark appointed her executive secretary of the Continuing Committee of the National Conference on Prevention and Control of Juvenile Delinquency. She and Jack shared a small house on 31st Street in the Georgetown section of Washington. Eunice did the cooking and Jack ate whatever she put before him. Both went to their offices in the morning and brought work home in the evening. Jack's was in a briefcase, but Eunice was usually accompanied by living case studies among the juvenile delinquents with whom she was working. The house could accommodate five or six of them, but when the delinquent girls numbered more than seven, Jack usually invited all of them, including Eunice, out to dinner.

Eunice was tall, slender, attractive and in her mid-twenties then. Brother and sister could each do an enormous amount of work, driving their office forces to the limit, and yet they were known as being among the most placid and tranquil persons in Washington. When juvenile delinquents were not invited, the house became a popular place for dinner and a gathering of friends for unending conversations and games of gin rummy. There was only one complaint, phrased by Jack's friends this way: "If you stay at Jack's place overnight, you don't get a night cap. You get a glass of milk before going to bed." The Kennedys do not smoke or drink.

If either Jack or Eunice had a plane to catch for London, Paris, Rome or the Far East, they continued conversations with friends, unhurried and undisturbed as a frenzied secretary interrupted frequently, saying: "You've got only twenty-five minutes to make it," counting down to "twenty minutes," and "fifteen minutes," when either would pick up a bag with serene composure and walk out to a cab. They never missed one and yet neither ever seemed to be concerned.

Eunice became the Justice Department's liaison officer

to the National Conference on Juvenile Problems; to state agencies interested in the work and to private organizations. She devised a plan whereby state and community conferences could fight juvenile delinquency that was adopted by twenty-six governors and more than three hundred mayors. She felt then that the job was completed and in June, 1948, she resigned, but she was far from through with the problem. She would continue to spend years at it in various areas.

John F. Kennedy, as a fledgling Congressman, was assigned to the House Committee on Education and Labor, a surprising appointment for two reasons. It did not seem politically appropriate to place the son of one of the country's richest men on a committee on labor, and it was clear at the opening of Congress that this would be one of the most important committees of the session. He was also given a place on the District of Columbia Committee because he asked for it. He said that he wanted to familiarize himself with affairs of governmental operation.

His speaking engagements multiplied quickly after his election. He turned few of them down, and then only because of conflicts in dates. At the outset of the Christmas season before he went to Washington, his talk before three hundred Boston business leaders opened a series of luncheon lectures sponsored by the Lieutenant Joseph P. Kennedy Post, Veterans of Foreign Wars. He was named a month later, by the United States Chamber of Commerce, along with Arthur Schlesinger, Jr., Joe Louis, Bill Mauldin and others, as one of the outstanding men of the year 1947.

His youthful appearance in the House of Representatives during the first few months caused some embarrassment. Several of his colleagues mistook him for a page boy. Congressmen George Sarbacher of Pennsylvania and Marion T. Bennett of Missouri were having the same difficulty. An order was issued that page boys must wear knickerbockers; it was later rescinded, but the page boys were put into distinctive uniforms.

In one of the early hearings of the Labor Committee in March, 1947, Kennedy found himself confronting his former economics teacher at Harvard, Russ Nixon, in a curious turn-about — an ex-student cross-examining an ex-instructor in a bitter clash over Communism. Nixon was now the legislative representative of the CIO Electrical Workers Union. He acknowledged that some Communists were members of the union and defended their right to belong to the party and hold office if they were elected.

Kennedy drew from Nixon the comment: "I know the purpose of the Communists is to supplant capitalism with a form of socialism." Kennedy pressed him to reveal whether Julius Emspak, the union's treasurer, was a Communist. Nixon said that Emspak had testified before the Senate Labor Committee that he was not.

"For your information," Kennedy said, "he was a Communist and documentary proof will be provided."

Curiously enough, and in spite of the hard time Kennedy had given his former economics teacher, Nixon listed Kennedy as among the committee members who were favorable to labor. Kennedy inquired about a mysterious "Comrade Jupiter," reputed to be an important labor leader, and later asked for a number of perjury indictments, based partly upon the testimony of Louis Budenz, once high in the Communist party and later an anti-Communist.

A month later Kennedy established that Nixon was right in his estimate of him. Kennedy abhorred Communists, but he was the friend of labor. He criticized many of the "curb labor" features of legislation then pending in Congress in a minority opinion of a House report on labor union restrictions and filed an amendment leaving it to the Supreme Court to determine whether a strike imperils public safety and health.

He charged that the majority of the House committee who framed the "curb labor" legislation had succumbed completely to the old and deeply rooted anti-labor prejudices that had delayed for decades the development of a forthright, constructive labor policy in the United States. "The simple truth is," he said, "that management, labor and government — insofar as it is represented by the majority of the committee on labor and education — have failed in their responsibilities. . . . Management has been selfish. Labor has been selfish."

He approved of Post Office Department economy measures proposed in the Hoover Commission report; criticized New England businessmen for opposing and not supporting legislation advocated by Democratic administrations for sixteen years and designed to improve the economic condition of the country and stave off depressions, and applauded a bill to increase the minimum wage from forty to seventy-five cents an hour. Honors that he did not seek were showered upon him. He was made a Director-at-large of the Harvard Alumni Association and elected to the Board of Overseers of the Boston Boys' Clubs.

James Michael Curley, whom he had succeeded in Congress — then the Mayor of Boston — had been found guilty in federal court in Washington of using the mails to defraud. A petition for his pardon had been circulated by Congressman John McCormack, the Democratic whip. It had been signed by Representatives Philbin of Massachusetts, Knudsen of Minnesota, Hoffman of Michigan, Rankin of Mississippi, and Patman of Nevada; and Edith Nourse Rogers, Representative from Massachusetts, had indicated that she, too, would sign, but Kennedy refused.

In August, 1947, Kennedy and Representative Charles Kersten of Wisconsin decided to tour Europe to study labor conditions there, both paying their own expenses. They were interested in Communist infiltration into Italian, French and German trade unions; but at the same time Kennedy was not forgetting the voters back home. Even as he was leaving Boston airport, he addressed a crowd on hand for his departure, attacking the Republicans in Congress for "letting the veterans down in their critical housing problem" and dumping the rent increase problem in the laps of tenants in "a cheap political way."

Throughout the term, he was concerned about civilian defense; approved of the Marshall Plan and urged its enactment. He characterized it as the only hope for world peace. Although he was world-minded, he was also vote-minded enough even to ask for a review of the court-martial of a constituent sentenced to life in a federal prison. He made it a rule to be easily available. He maintained a fully staffed

Patrick J. Kennedy, first
American-born progenitor of
an expansive Kennedy line.
From an oil painting by F. B.
Conlin in the P. J. Kennedy
School in East Boston.

Mr. and Mrs. Joseph P. Kennedy

Washington Post Roto

Bachrach

Mr. and Mrs. Kennedy with their children in 1937. Left to right: Mr. Kennedy, Patricia, John F., Jean, Eunice, Robert, Kathleen, Edward, Rosemary, Joseph, Jr., and Mrs. Kennedy.

Joseph P. Kennedy, Sr.

Joe, Jr., training at Squantum in 1941

Bob and Jack at a committee hearing in Washington

Jack and Jackie at Hyannisport

office in Washington and another in the Post Office Building in Boston. The door was always open for any voter or friend to come in with any problem, get a hearing and immediate action or a yes or no decision. The voter never was left in doubt. Kennedy was spending far more than his salary giving this kind of service.

He had been trained by his father in London and in the newspaper business as a correspondent to ascertain and establish the facts by going to the source. He did so regardless of how long it would take, how much it would cost or the inconvenience entailed. He would fly to any place on earth to talk to a central figure, the persons involved, or those who ought to know the answers. Sometimes he made these transoceanic flights while on crutches and wearing a steel brace to support his back.

The opinions of Massachusetts political leaders were divided. To some, he was a young man going places in a hurry. Others felt that they had a bull by the tail and pondered whether to hang on or let go. In any case, a "draft Kennedy for Governor" movement was born early in 1948. It was gaining momentum when Kennedy scotched it. The time came to file nomination papers. The promoters were waiting for him to sign. They had all the required signatures from four counties, but Kennedy shook his head and filed for re-election to Congress. He did not campaign that year.

On Thursday night, May 13, 1948, Kathleen Kennedy Hartington was killed in an airplane crash in the South of France. Her father had been in Paris awaiting her. Jack and

Eunice were in Washington. Bob, then a student at Harvard, was in Italy. Patricia was in New York. Mrs. Kennedy was in Hot Springs, Arkansas.

Within a few days all of the Kennedys were assembled at a graveside in Derbyshire where the twenty-eight-year-old Marchioness of Hartington was buried in her husband's family plot.

The usual or standard procedure in political progress in Massachusetts is to climb the ladder of success to the Governor's chair one rung at a time, coming up through city politics from minor to major offices or through state politics via the legislature to the office of Speaker of the House or President of the Senate. If Kennedy could have been sidetracked to the Governorship, somebody else would have opposed Henry Cabot Lodge two years later. The Kennedy vote and victory made it clear that he must inevitably be that candidate and the procession to his bandwagon began on the accepted principle of politics that "if you can't lick 'em, join 'em."

While John F. was working his way onward and upward toward the United States Senate, his brother Robert was at Harvard playing end on the football team and was to go on from there to Virginia Law School. All of the girls were busy about various causes and projects. Of these, Eunice achieved a rare distinction in her field. She had become a poised speaker, particularly before women's groups and large audiences, and in May, 1950, she went to the Federal Reformatory for Women at Alderson, West Virginia, to spend a month inside its walls working on the problems of returning delinquent women to society after imprisonment.

For years she had known the warden, Miss Nina Kinsella of Salem, Massachusetts, formerly chief social worker with the Massachusetts Department of Correction. Miss Kinsella had recently been appointed to head the Alderson Reformatory. She held that a warden of a women's prison should know the full background of every woman within her charge in order to bring about her rehabilitation. Eunice Kennedy agreed, and when she left Alderson a month later she knew as much about all of the women there as could be learned; she had lived with them.

She was convinced that the public would do more to help if it knew more about them. She toured the country talking to women, pleading for another chance for released prisoners. She believed that the Alderson Reformatory had the answer; in her view it was a model institution, beautifully situated in the Blue Ridge Mountains, without bars, guards, or uniforms, where the prisoners wore gay-colored dresses and lived in cottages that faced what resembled a college campus.

She acknowledged that the cottage system of correction cost $1500 for every $900 spent in the old-fashioned, grim type of institution, but as against this, she argued, ninety per cent of the women released from Alderson never broke their parole.

Alderson, as she described it, was far from a women's country club. The administration enforced discipline and imposed punishments in its system of rehabilitation. "The way to get this plan started in your community," she explained, "is for a group of four or five women to get together and visit your nearest women's reformatory. Each woman should single out one to sponsor; see her for an hour or so each week; take the girl to lunch and a movie. Most of these girls come from broken homes. They have no one to turn to and that's why they need sponsors. Keep in touch with them after they are released. The support is not financial, but moral."

Eunice was by all odds the gayest and yet the most casual of the Kennedy girls. Like her sisters, she had a wardrobe crammed with Paris gowns, but she was happiest when banging around the house in Hyannisport wearing an old skirt and sweater and a pair of men's shoes she inherited from an old friend of her father.

Patricia is the economist and mathematician of the family, not exactly a bargain hunter, but one who demands full value for her money. Patricia is the only Kennedy daughter who accepted a salaried job. Like the other girls, she would have worked for nothing in any charity of her choice, but the only way she could learn a craft that intrigued and appealed to her was to work at it.

Her father's association with show business may have been responsible. She was attracted to it, but not as an actress. She preferred to work behind the scenes — to produce and direct — and had a definite idea of what she would do when she learned how.

Soon after she got her A.B. from Rosemont College in 1947, she went to work for the National Broadcasting

Company in its production department. She worked her way up as a production assistant and resigned in 1951 to go to California and join the Family Theater group of Father Patrick Peyton, C.S.J.

The Family Theater had a radio program every Wednesday night on the Mutual Network. Six or eight times a year on important days, such as Christmas, Easter, Lincoln's and Washington's Birthdays, the Family Theater presented, in addition to its radio shows, hour-long television shows. Patricia had a part in the preparation of the scripts and in the production of these shows for both radio and TV.

Jean Kennedy followed much the same pattern. She had attended public school in Bronxville, Maplehurst College of the Sacred Heart, the Convent of the Sacred Heart in Roehampton, England, while her father was Ambassador, and was graduated from the Noroton Convent of the Sacred Heart and the Manhattanville College of the Sacred Heart.

Soon after her graduation from Manhattanville, she went to Chicago to work in the department of public relations of the Merchandise Mart, one of her father's properties. She remained there for a year and a half. She felt then that she had absorbed enough to go into public relations for any charity that could use her services.

In the spring of 1951, Eunice was contemplating further studies of the juvenile delinquent mind. Jean was undecided about her future. Eunice tried to persuade Jean to join her in work, but Jean was uncertain. The two decided to take a trip to the Middle East. Both were interested in what was going on there.

Eunice managed to persuade the publisher of the *Boston Post* to engage her as a foreign correspondent and to provide her with the necessary journalistic credentials. It turned out well. She got an exclusive interview with Queen Frederika of Greece, then in the news, and her dispatches were well worth the newspaper's investment.

When they returned, Eunice and Jean joined the staff of the House of the Good Shepherd in Chicago, working as a team. Jean, though, had never been quite convinced that this was her forte. Eunice became the liaison officer with the Juvenile Court. Two weeks later Eunice and Jean were in an automobile with a sullen teen-age girl who grappled with them and tried to escape. The physical violence did not disturb Eunice. She had had experiences like this before, but Jean decided that this kind of work was for the tougher and more rugged. She left for New York to join Father James Keller, founder and director of the Christophers, an organization that needed a good public relations hand at that time.

The aims and objectives of the Christophers is to raise the standards of government, education, labor relations, literature and entertainment. In their own words, "because of neglect by the average good person, control of these spheres of influence often goes by default into the hands of those bent on corruption or subversion." The Christopher News Notes are sent monthly to more than a million persons, free of charge. The Christopher Books — nine of them — have a circulation of three million copies. Radio and television programs are broadcast each week. Jean helped Father Keller in all phases of this work as an editorial assistant.

Just as Jack had been under the shadow and influence of Joe, Jr., always in competition with him, so in some measure was Robert overshadowed by Jack, although he was not in competition with him in the same way, partly because the disparity in ages — nine years — was greater. Robert followed the Kennedy family tradition, played on the football team at Harvard and took time out to serve in the Navy as his brothers had. He enlisted in the Navy at the age of seventeen and deliberately chose to be an able-bodied seaman so that he could serve on the destroyer *Joseph P. Kennedy, Jr.* Robert, too, had idolized Joe. He could have waited a year or two and been enrolled in an officers' school, but no one in the family attempted to dissuade him from his decision. He served on the destroyer chiefly during the Korean War.

He returned to complete his course at Harvard, graduated with honors and enrolled as a law student in the University of Virginia. While there, he persuaded Supreme Court Justice William O. Douglas, a friend of the Kennedy family, to come to the University to deliver a lecture. Out of this grew a suggestion from one or the other that they go behind the Iron Curtain and explore all of the places in the Far East barred to Americans — Oriental and Central Asia, the southern portion of Turkestan. It would take four years of negotiation with Moscow before this would come to pass.

Bob, too, followed his brothers as a foreign correspondent. He was in the Middle East in 1948 to see the war in Palestine. He was such a frequent visitor to places like Beirut, Lebanon and Damascus in Syria that they had become as familiar to him as American cities.

In 1950, while Robert was still at the Virginia Law School, he married Ethel Skakel, daughter of the George Skakels of Greenwich, Connecticut. He had met her first in Chicago where her father had been exceptionally successful in the coal chemistry business. Ethel was a prize-winning swimmer and horsewoman. The first Kennedy wedding since Kathleen's was a full-dress affair with hundreds of guests. After the honeymoon, Bob returned to the Virginia Law School, from which he graduated the following year.

He was admitted to the Massachusetts Bar; admitted to practice before the United States Supreme Court and became an attorney in the Criminal Division of the Department of Justice in the same year.

Robert is quick and incisive, like his father, with a natural skill for investigation and interrogation. He has the ability to seize upon inconsistencies and dig into oral or written reports to clear away camouflage and expose facts. He is a good organizer and has a memory for details.

In 1951 he still found time to make a round-the-world tour with his brother Jack and his sister Patricia. He had made himself a skilled cameraman in black-and-white and color. He had spent part of 1949 in Europe with occasional forays behind the Iron Curtain, trying to get into Hungary to tell the story of the arrest of Joseph Cardinal Mindszenty for the Hearst papers — and was balked. He got it eventually from Hungarians who had managed to get into Austria.

≈§ 13 §≈

DURING THE SPRING and summer of 1952, all of the Kennedys, father, mother and the full roster of children were gathered in Massachusetts. On April 8, John F. Kennedy had announced that he would contest for the seat of Henry Cabot Lodge in the United States Senate. His announcement was short and concise. "There is not only a crisis abroad," he said, "but there is a crisis in Massachusetts. Our citizens who are out of work can testify to that. Our competitive position with other states has been weakened. Unemployment, particularly in our textile and shoe centers, is on the increase." He went on to say that industries and jobs had disappeared because the Senators from Massachusetts had done nothing about it. "Other states have vigorous leaders in the Senate to defend the interests of their people," he concluded, "and Massachusetts needs the same kind of leadership."

The Kennedys were well financed. They were indefatigable campaign workers. It seemed as if they never slept. They were out early and late. They had no disdain for tiresome, tedious, menial jobs, and no respect for shoe leather. They behaved as though each one, individually, was responsible for Jack's election or defeat. It was the first experience of Massachusetts Republicans with the united Kennedy front. They did not know how to combat it. They knew they were in for a hard fight.

Henry Cabot Lodge had spread himself thin. He was a candidate for the United States Senate and at the same time he was managing Eisenhower's campaign for the Presidency. The Kennedys could cover a tremendous amount of ground with amazing speed and they could get things done before the opposition knew what it was about.

Within three weeks of his announcement, four thousand women had responded to engraved invitations to attend a reception and tea given by Mrs. Joseph P. Kennedy in the Worcester Sheraton Hotel. Hundreds of women had been called personally on the telephone by Mrs. Kennedy and her daughters. Within three hours each of the four thousand had shaken hands with a Kennedy.

Joseph P. Kennedy moved into Boston's Ritz-Carlton. Democratic politicians of the state beat a pathway to his door. Robert dropped everything to manage his brother's campaign. They started early, worked late and never ceased. Women's committees grew like mushrooms across the state. John F. Kennedy, tousle-haired, handsome, popped up to address them at meetings everywhere. They loved him and mothered him.

The Kennedy girls, pretty, gay and smiling, captivated male audiences. They wore skirts with the words "Vote for John F. Kennedy" embroidered in script on the front.

When they were not speaking in public, they were going through precincts, wards, cities, towns and villages, ringing doorbells, introducing themselves to the woman of the house: "I am John Kennedy's sister. May I come in?" All of them had taken six months' leave from their current activities and occupations. Eunice abandoned her juvenile delinquency activities. Patricia, who had been working at NBC on the Kate Smith hour, left her job. Jean took temporary leave.

They went from house to house in rain or shine; cajoling suspicious dogs, visiting supermarkets, housing projects, talking to any woman or women who would listen. During the evening they attended rallies and circulated among audiences when the speaking had ended. They followed assiduously their father's injunction: "If a job is worth doing, it's worth doing well."

The Republican State Committee was confounded and bewildered by this technique. Lodge's workers were smothered. There were too many Kennedys and they were everywhere, even outside the mill gates in Lowell, Lawrence and Fall River. The Kennedys made headlines without half trying. Jack, on the platform, was always the perfect gentleman, very articulate in dissecting Candidate Lodge without giving him anything worth answering on page one.

Kennedy preached the political and economic philosophy of Franklin Delano Roosevelt. He believed the American people wanted to adhere to it, as had a majority of voters in Massachusetts for twenty years. He acknowledged that neither the Democratic party nor its record was entirely perfect, but that the voters would not, nevertheless, tolerate a change. He expressed it then as he saw it: "The Democratic party is the party which cares for people. It is the party of imagination and compassion. It is the party which thinks that unemployment is intolerable. It is the party committed to the proposition that we are not helpless before the sterile, abstract laws which constitute the economic creed of reaction. It is the party which believes that our great resources and industrial skills must be directed into channels where they serve not the interests of the fiscally mighty, but the simple needs of the common man.

"I do not want to see social decency compromised, or human passion forgotten. I want a better life for every American. I want to see every American walk with his head up . . . secure as far as possible against misfortunes that are not of his own making . . . and confident that he can provide his children with opportunities for a fuller and more useful life . . . This is my political creed."

By the middle of August in 1952, Congressman Kennedy had spoken in 311 of the 351 cities and towns that make up the state of Massachusetts. He had addressed the Masons, Eagles, Rangers, Rotary, Kiwanis, Knights of Columbus. He had spoken at college graduation exercises and conventions of steel workers, carpenters and garment workers and before racial groups and organizations of Ukrainians, Swedes and Latvians.

Requests for him to speak were pouring in at the rate of fifty to sixty a week. He employed no ghost writers. He authored his own speeches either in writing or by dictating them to Helen Doyle, his secretary. Over a period of eighteen months he had averaged six or seven speeches a day and more on weekends, and once broke his own record by appearing before eight groups on one Saturday.

During the month of July in 1952, five Sunday teas and receptions were given in his honor in Worcester, Springfield, Quincy, Fitchburg and Taunton, and at these teas he met and had conversations with fifteen thousand women — not merely exchanges of greetings but time-consuming chats.

Throughout all of this, he never missed a roll call in Congress. He was there on all Tuesday, Wednesday and Thursday voting days, commuting by plane or train between Washington and Boston. While traveling, he read books or wrote speeches. He never boarded a train or plane without reading material. In the course of a week he read six daily newspapers, seven weekly magazines and four to six books.

It normally takes about six minutes to walk from Kennedy's apartment on Beacon Hill to his office in the Boston Post Office Building. As the campaign progressed, it took longer and longer for him to cover the distance. He was stopped by so many people who wanted to shake hands and talk with him that he was forced to use a cab.

From 7:30 in the morning until midnight and after, this was the routine of a candidate and campaigner with a bad back that sometimes kept him in excruciating pain, although he never revealed it.

The contest between Henry Cabot Lodge and John F. Kennedy for the United States Senate in 1952 was a gentlemanly political duel, unusual in the state of Massachusetts, where candidates customarily slug it out with insults and bitter criticisms. Long before election Kennedy was, in the jargon of the day, "home free." Every Democratic leader of importance, and scores of no importance, had climbed upon his bandwagon, either by enthusiastic choice or in self-defense. Early in September the odds quoted by Boston gamblers on Kennedy to win were ten to one. They would climb to twenty to one. He could not lose.

Influential Republicans, unsatisfied with Lodge, were bolting to Kennedy, although they did not call it that. Basil Brewer, publisher of the *New Bedford Standard*, disappointed when Robert A. Taft was not chosen by the Republican convention as a candidate for President, endorsed Kennedy — a surprise to both candidates.

Kennedy was the aggressor. He raised issues that put Lodge on the defensive. Because of his service in the Embassy in London and his wide travel throughout the Continent and Asia, Kennedy was familiar with foreign affairs, but Lodge was equally well equipped. Throughout 1950 and until the summer of 1951, Kennedy had supported all Marshall Plan aid, but he became convinced that there was a waste in foreign aid spending and in August, 1951, he had voted for a $350,000,000 cut in economic aid to Europe during consideration of the 1952 Mutual Security Bill.

He favored admitting more refugees to the United States and endorsed a bill providing for the issuance of 300,000 special non-quota immigration visas for Italy, persons of German ethnic origin and Greece. He had argued in Congress and in his public speeches that no progress in civil rights legislation could be made unless filibusters in the Senate could be prevented, and proposed a change in Senate rules permitting cloture of debate by a majority of the Senators present.

On nomination day, in September, when neither candidate had an opponent within his party at the polls, the Waltham League of Women Voters arranged a debate between Lodge and Kennedy. The South Junior High School was jammed with twelve hundred, and more hundreds were turned away. Mrs. Harvey Karp presided and Saville Davis, a Boston newspaper editor, was moderator. He had very little to moderate. Both Lodge and Kennedy were mild, affable, agreeable and to some extent praised each other. It was no Lincoln-Douglas affair. An audience who came for verbal fireworks sat through an hour of peaceful discussion and dissertation. The two candidates agreed on too many things. They disagreed chiefly over the Korean policy and who should be Senator from Massachusetts.

Kennedy defended Truman's administration, although he admitted that some serious errors in judgment had been made. He charged that the Republican party was divided; its hard core in the Midwest still clinging fondly to the belief that the United States had faced no revolution and that its lines of defense still began on the two great oceans. "They bemoan the losses in the Far East," he said, "yet they are reluctant to support policies that may save the rest of Asia and the Middle East."

He went on to say that the Republican party's "coastal fringes," sensing something new and mysterious loose in the world, were clinging to the coattails of the Democrats in the hope of imitating their political success. "What hope for a better world," he asked, "lies in the leadership of a party which has opposed so much progressive legislation, foreign and domestic, during the past twenty years?" He discussed seven issues: inflation, social welfare, labor, civil rights, the tidelands, corruption and foreign affairs. He was scathing in his criticism of the Republican voting record on social welfare and labor legislation, but on civil rights, although he was bitterly critical of the Republicans, he praised Lodge.

When it was over, a man in the audience summed it up for a reporter. He said, "I liked both of them."

Throughout the rest of the barnstorming campaign, this gentlemanly, kid-glove treatment of each other continued, to the astonishment of voters, who, merely by turning a knob on a radio or television set, could see and hear other candidates for state offices vilifying each other. Although Kennedy did not attack Lodge, he "reminded" the voters that Lodge had been absent on forty-five out of forty-six roll calls during his last session in the Senate; that he had been absent during the McCarran Act showdown; that he had voted five times to weaken and nullify rent controls. He then called for development of new industries in Massachusetts to take up the slack in the cities that depended almost entirely on the manufacture of shoes and textiles.

Lodge seemed to be too busy managing Eisenhower's campaign to answer Kennedy or to present a program of his own to reduce unemployment in the state.

Throughout the campaign Kennedy had never mentioned or even indirectly referred to his service in the Navy. When questioned about it from the floor at any rally, he slid over it lightly and dismissed it in a few sentences. Almost any other Democratic candidate for any office in Massachusetts would have shouted it from the rooftops and exploited it to the limit.

In mid-October, at the height of the campaign, Kennedy received a letter which surprised and pleased him so much that he released it to the press. It received widespread newspaper attention. This is it:

166 KOFUNE, UBADO-MURE
YAMAGUN, FUKUSHIMA-KEN
JAPAN

THE HONORABLE JOHN F. KENNEDY
THE UNITED STATES CONGRESS
WASHINGTON, D. C.
U. S. A.

DEAR MR. KENNEDY:

I am informed by Dr. Gungi Hosono that a warship sunk by a destroyer of the Japanese Navy during the Solomon Islands Battle in August, 1943, was under your command. This is a big surprise to me as I happened to be the Commander of the destroyer which sank your ship. When I read the Time Magazine of August 18, 1952, which mentioned the battle in question, my memory being refreshed, I can vividly recall what happened at that time.

Now allow me to take this opportunity to tell you about myself. I had been a destroyer commander since October, 1940. In view of an international crisis at that time, the Imperial Japanese Navy was prepared for the worst while attaching the last hope in the eventual success of the American-Japanese diplomatic talk. As even we young officers were quite aware of the risk in fighting the combined force of the United States and British navies with our inferior naval strength, the attack on Pearl Harbor, which was entirely secret to us, therefore seriously disturbed us.

While most of our naval officers except the war-like minority were naturally pessimistic about the outcome of the war, the unexpected victory at the commencement of the war and the skillful propaganda of General Tojo's cabinet led us to entertain a wishful thinking for the chance of victory. Following our defeat at the Midway Islands, however, the whole situation changed against Japan and became favorable to the United States, which displayed tremendously the strength of the war political and the fighting spirit.

I was engaged in the battle of the Solomon Islands following the seizure of Laboul (New Britain Islands). I was very much concerned with the situation which was then further aggravated by the successive defeat in the Battle of Guadalcanal.

From Nov. 1942 to May 1943, I was assigned to the duty in the Track Islands water. It was early June, 1943. I was transfered to Laboul again as the commander of the destroyer Amagiri. From that time the counter-attack of the American force became increasingly offensive. As Americans controlled the air, we were in no more position to attack in the daytime and we had to operate at night, attempting in vain to prevent, by destroyer force, the transportation of American men and munitions.

We met the disastrous defeat in Kure in early June when our flagship was instantly sunk in the first encounter with your fleet, equipped with radar (which we were not aware) and this was followed by the subsequent defeat with the result that we were forced to retreat to Laboul after the series of unsuccessful battles.

In one of the night battles in early August, 1943, I sighted a bold enemy boat of small size. It was heading directly toward my detroyer of larger type. Having no time to exchange gunfires as ships came so close to each other, my destroyer had to directly hit the enemy boat, slicing in two. To my great surprise, this boat happened to be the PT boat which was under your command.

I take this opportunity to pay my profound respect to your daring and courageous action in this battle and also to congratulate you upon your miraculous escape under such circumstances.

In my country the election is being held at present for the Diet members. I do wish the best of your success in the coming election in your country.

With personal regards,

Sincerely yours,
KOHEI HANAMI
Former Commander
of the Destroyer *Amagiri*

As the campaign drew to a close, its tempo was stepped up. Kennedy and Lodge continued to hammer at each other's records, but neither would attack the integrity of the other. One night, while campaigning in South Boston, Kennedy and Lodge found their cars abreast of each other. Lodge leaned out the window of his car, grinned and called to Kennedy. "Jack! Isn't this a hell of a way to make a living?" Kennedy smiled and nodded as the cars pulled away.

Eisenhower came to Boston the day before election to lend his weight in a final speech in crowded Boston Garden to put Lodge over, the ultimate in help that the party could give, but it was too little and too late. When the votes were counted Eisenhower had swept the state, but Kennedy defeated Lodge, 1,207,105 votes to 1,138,352. Kennedy was the only successful Democrat in the top echelon of the ticket.

While Kennedy celebrations were going on here and there in Boston, the scene within the Curley house on Jamaicaway was hardly one of gaiety. The former Governor who had hoped one day to become a United States Senator was surrounded by his cronies. They had been following the returns on television and Curley knew now that the curtain had fallen on the long play of his political career. Never again would he wield the power and authority he had once held.

His close friend, Governor Paul Dever, had been defeated by Republican Christian Herter. Curley's support had done Dever no good. The fair-haired boy in the Massachusetts Democratic party was now John F. Kennedy.

Curley had had no part in the Kennedy campaign. He had not been consulted. He had been ignored, compelled to give his silent support entirely because he could not run out on the Democratic nominee, and so the third Kennedy in the line of succession now defrauded him of a good fight. He could not even oppose him at the convention.

The Kennedy campaign had had everything in it, including some touches that Curley himself would have relished. The realization that his future was now empty must have been very painful. The Mayor's office had always been his refuge, but two years earlier he had been defeated by John B. Hynes. He had campaigned then on the slogan "The Spirit of '76." There seemed to be little now to look forward to.

The Kennedys had become a political dynasty. Curley would have no successor to carry on his name. Kennedy had had nine children, now reduced to seven. Curley had

had eight, now reduced to two. Two of his daughters had died in infancy; three of his sons in early manhood, including James Michael, Jr., who resembled him and might have followed in his footsteps. Leo, a promising lawyer, who might have become a political figure, had found his sister Mary dead in her apartment, victim of a heart attack. The shock was too much; he died of a heart attack while telephoning for a doctor to attend her.

Francis, who had inherited his father's wit, his sense of timing, his golden voice, and his genius for the precise word or phrase, had put these talents to a different use — he joined the Jesuit order. The interests of George, his youngest, were turned elsewhere and he was temperamentally unsuited to politics. There could be none to carry on the name.

❦ 14 ❦

EUNICE KENNEDY was married in May, 1953, to Robert Sargent Shriver, Jr., by Cardinal Spellman at an impressive ceremony in New York's St. Patrick's Cathedral.

A month earlier, just before Easter time, she and her sisters went to Paris by plane to pick out her trousseau. Mrs. Kennedy could not get away at the moment and cabled the girls that she would join them. She was delayed. Before she got there, her daughters had become weary of Paris and hopped off for Marrakech in French Morocco for a holiday.

Mrs. Kennedy arrived to find they had gone. She cabled that she was coming right over to Marrakech. They dropped everything to rush to the airport. She arrived in a Comet jet that had covered the distance in a matter of minutes. As she alighted, the girls looked on open-mouthed and horrified. They themselves had been afraid to fly in it, but their mother was not concerned about the experience; she wanted to know about the wedding gown.

It was the first wedding and the first nuptial Mass ceremony to be performed by the Cardinal for anyone outside of his immediate family since his elevation to ecclesiastical status in 1946. The couple received the Apostolic Blessing from the Pope via the Papal Delegate in Washington.

It was a beautiful and impressive ceremony, a pageant of grandeur and splendor that, in blasé, ceremony-surfeited New York, brought five to seven thousand curious spectators to St. Patrick's Cathedral. More than seventeen hundred guests gathered at the reception held on the Starlight Roof of the Waldorf-Astoria. So many dignitaries were there from the United States and foreign countries that the list of their names might have made up *Who's Who*.

Robert Sargent Shriver, Jr., the groom, better known to his friends as "Sarge," was born in Westminster, Maryland. His father was vice-president of the Baltimore Trust Company and later a New York investment banker. He prepared at Canterbury School in New Milford, Connecticut, went on to Yale and was graduated *cum laude*. He continued on to the Yale Law School for his LL.B. degree. During World War II he served as a gunnery officer on the U.S.S. *South Dakota* in engagements at Guadalcanal, the Central Pacific and with the British fleet at Scapa Flow, after which he attended the Submarine School in New London, Connecticut, and served three years with the submarine force in the Pacific.

He returned to civilian life to join the editorial department of *Newsweek*, where he became assistant to the editorial director. He resigned in 1948 to join the Joseph P. Kennedy Enterprises as assistant general manager of the

Merchandise Mart in Chicago. He first met Eunice when he was loaned to her by her father to assist her in her work among the juvenile delinquents of Chicago.

Whether through natural choice, the politically contagious atmosphere of the Kennedy family or indoctrination, after marriage Sarge Shriver became interested in Chicago politics and found himself on the first stepping-stone as President of the Chicago Board of Education.

Four months after Eunice's wedding, Senator John F. Kennedy became a bridegroom. Soon after he was seated as a Senator, he met Jacqueline Lee Bouvier at a dinner party at the home of a Washington correspondent, Charles Bartlett. She was twenty-two years old then; the Senator, thirty-five. Kennedy, as a newspaperman, had been a foreign correspondent for the Hearst papers and covered the founding meeting of the United Nations in San Francisco. He was then working for the Chicago *Herald-Examiner*. Later, he covered the Potsdam Conference for International News Service. Jacqueline was a news photographer.

She has been described as a cameo beauty with a manner that is soft, almost shy. This may have accounted for her unusual success as an inquiring reporter-photographer for the Washington *Times-Herald*.

She was born July 28, 1930, in fashionable Southampton, Long Island, the daughter of the John V. Bouviers; her father was a member of the New York Stock Exchange. She had had an extensive education; went to Miss Chapin's school in Manhattan, Holton Arms in Washington, Miss Porter's School in Farmington, Connecticut, Vassar, the

Sorbonne in Paris, George Washington University and finished by taking the foreign service course at Georgetown.

She won a fashion magazine contest that entitled her to a year's work in Paris but turned it down at the suggestion of Arthur Krock of the *New York Times*, whom she had told about it at a dinner one night; he had suggested the newspaper business instead.

She thereupon applied for a job at the *Times-Herald*, where she was told that the paper did not need reporters, but photographers.

"I'm an experienced photographer," she bluffed.

She was hired and set about making good the bluff. She thumbed through the yellow pages of the telephone directory, found a camera school in Southeast Washington. When she got there she discovered that it was a Negro school, but that did not deter her. She was given a quick, almost overnight course in how to snap a picture. In the beginning the instructor set a press camera at ten feet for her, gave her a few arbitrary stop numbers for light conditions and cautioned her to take all of her pictures at ten feet until he could give her more lessons.

Within a few weeks she had mastered enough of the technique to get away with it and perhaps, because she was so pretty, the picture editor winked at some of her work and even gave her some pointers. It was not long before the picture and city editors discovered that Jacqueline did not need the camera. She had a talent for sketching and was turned loose to do pen-and-ink human interest drawings, which became quite a feature of the paper.

Jack and Jacqueline were married on September 12, 1953, in the most spectacular wedding in Newport in three decades.

When they returned from the honeymoon, George Dixon, the widely syndicated Washington columnist, who had known Jacqueline in the early days when she was masquerading as a columnist, recalled a newspaper picture he had seen of her, posed nautically in a sailboat with the Senator. The caption described her as a great sailing enthusiast.

"How come, Jackie?" Dixon asked.

"Oh," Jacqueline answered. "My husband is the sailing enthusiast. They just shoved me into that boat long enough to take the picture."

Jacqueline still had a lot to learn about the Kennedys. She was to become a sailing enthusiast in time and learn a lot about sports and games she had never played before marriage. A time would come when she would break a leg playing football in Hyannisport.

During the first year of his married life, Senator Jack and his wife faced a situation that confronts few newly married couples. The back injury he had sustained in the Pacific still plagued him. A steel plate had been inserted in his back, and the wound over it had never healed. Most of the time he was on crutches. He had the kind of physical courage it takes to ignore it. He never complained or acknowledged to anyone that he was in pain. The only indication to his friends that he was suffering was that, occasionally, his face looked drawn.

Although he had no voice in foreign affairs, his interest

was so deep that he took a plane to Italy while he was on crutches, merely to satisfy his own curiosity about questions concerning foreign aid that puzzled him. His father, mother, sisters and brothers first learned of it when they read of it in the newspapers.

Another member of the family was soon to marry. Patricia Kennedy first met actor Peter Lawford during the Christmas holidays of 1952 when both were in Palm Beach. It was a casual meeting — not love at first sight. She met him occasionally after that in New York and Hollywood, since both were in show business. She was still associated with Father Patrick Peyton's Family Theater and the Family Rosary Crusade on TV and in radio. Lawford's name had been frequently linked with the daughter of another American Ambassador, Sharmen Douglas. Much of this was the work of studio press agents who would link romantically the names of any girl and actor escort if they were seen together at the same lunch table.

Lawford is the son of the late Lieutenant Sir Sidney Lawford and Lady Lawford. Sir Sidney served with the Royal Fusilliers Regiment as a captain in the Boer War and as a general in World War I. Lady Lawford also came of an Army family. Peter had come to the United States in 1937, determined to become an actor, and went to Hollywood, where he worked as a parking lot attendant and motion picture house usher until he finally made the grade at Metro-Goldwyn-Mayer studios; during the next ten years he starred in such productions as *Easter Parade*, *Royal Wedding*, and Columbia's *It Should Happen to You*.

Peter began to see Patricia much more frequently. Until that time he had been an evangelist preaching single blessedness and the virtues of bachelorhood. But the two-months courtship was interrupted when Patricia decided to accompany her brothers Jack and Bob around the world. She had a specific assignment to examine particularly the United States Information Service and the effectiveness of the Voice of America in the countries they visited.

What Peter and Patricia talked about just before she took off on the world flight, what arrangements they had made or the circumstances of parting remained a private matter. The Kennedys never discuss their private affairs in public and are rarely found in gossip columns. In any case, it is known that Peter called Patricia by telephone in Tokyo and he was waiting for her when she arrived in San Francisco. Soon they were on their way to see her father, who had to be told before they made it public.

As the husband of a Kennedy, Peter has made good in every particular, but there were some doubts and reservations in the beginning. When Lawford finally asked Joseph P. Kennedy for his daughter's hand, he was told:

"Peter, if there's anything I think I'd hate as a son-in-law, it's an actor; and if there's anything I think I'd hate worse than an actor as a son-in-law, it's an English actor."

Peter grinned — he understood. He congratulated his future father-in-law for being so honest and, perhaps from that moment, he got along fine with all of the other Kennedys and their in-laws.

Their engagement was announced, and all religious barriers to the marriage were removed by Peter's becoming a

Catholic. They were married on April 25 in the Church of St. Thomas More on Park Avenue and 59th Street, New York. Patricia therefore became the second Kennedy daughter to marry into a titled family. Lawford had recently become an American citizen.

This was a quiet afternoon wedding devoid of the panoply that had characterized earlier Kennedy weddings, and the reception at the Plaza Hotel was for members of the families and intimate friends only.

Mr. and Mrs. Lawford went to Hawaii on their honeymoon before making their home in California. Mrs. Lawford continued to work for the Family Theater and as chairman of the Democratic Digest of the State of California. On April 5, 1955, a son, Christopher, was born to her — the fifth grandchild of the Joseph P. Kennedys.

The Lawfords fit very nicely into the Kennedy scheme of things. They gather with the rest of the clan at Hyannisport in the summer and at Palm Beach during part of the winter. Peter is athletic, likes to participate in sports and games. Patricia inherited her father's comprehension of finance, is agile about figures, knows her way around in stocks and bonds and is perceptive about contracts and agreements. She sees to it that Peter gets all that is coming to him from all revenue sources, handles his accounts and sees to it that his obligations are met, including those to the income tax collector. They are a well-paired couple.

◄§ 15 §►

KENNEDY'S RECORD AS A CONGRESSMAN
satisfied most of the folks back home on many measures
and nettled some on occasions when he asserted his independence and deliberately risked offending them on issues
he knew to be unpopular. A hard core of loyal Curley followers could not forget that he had refused to sign the
petition asking executive clemency for Curley when he
was serving a term in the Federal Penitentiary in Danbury,
Connecticut, for using the mails to defraud.

In Massachusetts politics, metropolitan Boston is the tail
that wags the dog, and Kennedy knew the vote-getting
power that could be generated by public sympathy for
Curley whether in or out of jail, but he could not justify
such an action nor reconcile it with his principles. He preferred to risk unpopularity.

During the same year, he was the first Congressman in
the history of the state to support the frequently recurring
St. Lawrence Seaway bill, always unpopular in Massachusetts because of the economic damage it would do to the

Port of Boston. Foster Furcolo was a candidate for the Senate that year against Republican Leverett Saltonstall. Furcolo was popular in western Massachusetts, and strong enough throughout the state to be elected Governor two years later. Nevertheless, Kennedy's hands-off attitude was responsible in some measure for the re-election of Saltonstall. In the spring of the following year, John Lynch, Kennedy's candidate for Chairman of the Democratic State Committee, defeated the incumbent, William H. Burke, Jr., backed by the House Democratic Majority Leader, John W. McCormack.

Kennedy went along with the Democratic leadership on taxes, immigration, welfare programs and labor legislation. He voted for government development of the Niagara and Hell's Canyon power sites and against the Upper Colorado reclamation site. He backed foreign aid programs and generally favored a higher level of defense spending than the Eisenhower administration proposed. Throughout his term he supported the Democratic position on about two-thirds of the votes in which Republican and Democratic majorities took sides. This is about average for a Democratic Congressman.

He deviated from his party on farm policy. He voted consistently for the Administration's flexible farm price support plan and against the rigid ninety-percent props backed by most Democrats. In 1955, he was the only Democratic Senator to vote for the President's highway program. Earlier, he had voted with his party's majority against a "public preference" clause in atomic energy contracts and for a cut in TVA funds.

His record in the United States Senate during 1952 and 1953 could not hurt him back home. He had the woolen textile tariff raised, urged the President to obtain an agreement with Japan to cut textile imports, which was done; introduced a resolution to investigate the whole textile situation which passed; amended the Mutual Security Act limiting cotton textile imports; amended the Flammable Fabrics Act, which resulted in the saving of several New England mills; favored the Walsh-Healey woolen minimum wage to prevent Southern substandard competition, got low tariffs on raw wool imports and introduced a bill to prevent excessive speculation on raw wool which also passed.

He did right by the Massachusetts fishing industry by establishing fishing research and market development. His bill to reorganize the Fish and Wildlife Service, introduced in conjunction with Senator Saltonstall, provided a ten-million-dollar loan fund for fishermen. Both Senators cooperated to bring about passage of the Fishing Boat Protection Bill. The Boston Army Base Pier was given a ten-million-dollar rehabilitation job.

He brought federal construction to the Quincy Fore River Shipyard; urged appropriate watch tariff protection for Waltham; helped make New England factories available for atomic projects. He was on the right side for Massachusetts flood control, hurricane protection and tornado relief. Few constituents could complain about his record.

After six months as a Senator, as the summer recess approached, Kennedy contemplated a difficult decision. He had first injured his back playing football at Harvard. He had aggravated the injury further during the rescue operation in the Pacific; this difficulty was further complicated by recurrent malaria. A year earlier he had campaigned throughout Massachusetts, half the time on crutches. He was still on crutches while in the Senate. For a man of his disposition and temperament, this was awkward, embarrassing and the kind of handicap that made him unbearably unhappy. He yearned for good health, complete mobility, the ability to play games, sail a boat, drive an automobile and engage in sports.

He talked to the best specialists, spent days in the country's foremost clinics. All who examined him were dubious. He was told that success could be achieved only by a delicate operation to fuse several of the vertebrae in his spine. This was so dangerous that one noted specialist refused to undertake it and told him that he could not survive. Another told him that he would have only one chance in sixteen of coming through such an operation.

Kennedy decided to risk his life to regain some semblance of the health that he had once enjoyed. His decision placed an unenviable responsibility upon Dr. Philip D. Wilson and his assistants, and would require a confinement of two or three months. The operation was postponed ten times while doctors and surgeons continued to study X rays and make further tests. Convalescence was slow and tedious. In all he was out of action for eight months. He entered the New York Hospital for Special Surgery on October 11, 1954. A preliminary operation was performed, and on December 21 he left the hospital on a stretcher and was flown to Palm Beach to spend the Christmas season with the assembled Kennedys.

He re-entered the hospital on February 10, 1955. A metal plate and a screw were removed from his back. He was flown to Florida again to convalesce at the Kennedy place. He remained quartered there, being flown to New York for occasional clinical checkups, and was well on the way to full recovery when a defective crutch collapsed under him; the fall set him back several days.

As a relief from boredom during the long convalescence he decided to write a book he had been contemplating, presenting the most courageous Senators in the history of Congress. He kept his secretaries in Washington and Boston busy raiding libraries and shipping him biographical material.

The book was titled *Profiles in Courage*. It became a best-seller and won the Pulitzer Prize as well. In January, 1958, a television audience from coast to coast, watching the Mike Wallace show, heard Drew Pearson make the astonishing and incredible statement that *Profiles in Courage* had been written by one of Senator Kennedy's ghost writers.

The following week the president of the network came before the same cameras and microphones to apologize to Kennedy for the statement. Every visitor to the hospital and to the Kennedy house in Palm Beach, and there were hundreds of them, as well as the secretary who had transcribed his dictation, knew that the book had been written (or, more accurately, dictated and rewritten) by John F.

Kennedy himself. A superficial check would have established it.

In July, Kennedy celebrated his complete recovery by hiring a special train to take two hundred and eighty members of the Massachusetts legislature to his father's house in Hyannisport where he demonstrated his return to health by going through a strenuous day of softball, golf and swimming. The pain had entirely gone.

He had risked his life on a sixteen-to-one shot, and once again, he had won.

An unsung heroine of his ordeal was Jacqueline. She had never left his side from the day he entered the hospital. She sat by his bed day after day. She attended him when he was moved on a stretcher from hospital to plane and plane to house. She was with him on his trips to Washington. She helped him into and out of bed, put on his socks and slippers when he could not bend, assisted him to sit down at a table and to get up. She spent all of her hours with him.

The Senator summed her up in the words: "She's terrific!"

The sons and daughters of Joseph P. Kennedy are not interested in money per se. Each is a millionaire; their father saw to that years ago when he set up trust funds in their names. They were trained from childhood for public service, and their avowed and dedicated purpose is to do the most good with their money while they are here. A Kennedy cannot gauge his success by how much he earns. The only yardstick in the family is: "What have you accomplished?"

Of all the children, Robert resembles his father most closely, and is inclined to agree with him more often than the rest, although he is not necessarily influenced by him. Robert talks much like his father. He has the same incisive inflection, the same facility for going right to the heart of the matter, the same skill for organization. The Kennedys have differing opinions on many issues and subjects and these are respected within the family. Each is an individualist. They disagree, but if they cannot compromise, they never dispute about it. "That's what he thinks," or "that's what she thinks" is a common phrase among all of them, including father and mother.

All of the Kennedys have dogged determination and the same compelling will to win, but Bobby's goes a little bit deeper and it is obvious that at times he exerts more influence over the rest of the family than they do over him. His father once observed in a revealing moment that "Bobby could be depended upon to keep them in line," not that there was any possibility that one might stray from the line, but Bobby is the team's best quarterback. In any sudden and unexpected play he would call the right signals instinctively. Both the Senator and Robert were chosen at different times as among the ten outstanding young men in the United States. It is significant that it is Robert who is the president of the Joseph P. Kennedy, Jr., Foundation, which distributes more than $1,500,000 for hospitals, schools and charities every year.

All of the Kennedys are athletes — idle only when they sleep, and they seem to do very little of that. Regardless of age or sex, they are always in competition when they foregather at Hyannisport or Palm Beach, and that includes wives and husbands. Bobby never rejects a dare and sometimes dares himself; he is always proving that he can do almost anything. His wife Ethel remembers a day when they were driving through Sun Valley. Bobby saw a difficult ski slide and wondered if he could master it. "That was all he needed," she said. "He dropped everything to try it and almost broke his neck." It was on a ski slope on Mt. Tremblant in Canada, incidentally, that the pair met.

Touch football is a favorite sport among them, including the girls and in-laws. One who marries a Kennedy must be rugged. One time Bobby was so intent upon a touchdown that he ran headlong into a barbed wire fence and was thrown back, his face covered with blood. Ethel once summed him up this way: "Bob doesn't always have as good form as some of the other players, but he is so determined about it that the other side gets to feel that they never can beat him, and if you're on his side you feel you can't lose." The Senator once paid her the compliment of telling a friend: "Ethel's really good. You ought to see her run and pass."

Ethel had been Jean Kennedy's roommate at the College of the Sacred Heart in Manhattanville. She, too, had brothers and sisters — six of them — and they, too, were all athletic, but not to the same degree as the Kennedys.

Jack's wife Jacqueline feels just as strongly about the Senator as an athlete and game-player. "Once in a while," she complained, "when the Kennedys are playing Monopoly after a big day of outdoor sports, I make a mistake deliberately to end the game."

"Does Jack mind?" she was asked.

She smiled and her eyes sparkled. "Not if I'm on the other side," she said.

A guest at the Kennedy summer home in Hyannisport, who prefers to remain nameless, exhausted and debilitated after a weekend, once drew up a set of rules for visitors. The Kennedy clan found it so amusing and entertaining that it has been preserved and it is displayed on appropriate occasions. It is generally titled "What to Expect When Visiting the Kennedys."

It has this foreword:

The following ought to be placed under the pillow of each new guest and some of the old ones who may have forgotten. It should be read carefully. Failure to do so may cause you painful embarrassment.

AT THE DINNER TABLE

Prepare yourself by reading The Congressional Record, U.S. News & World Report, Time, Newsweek, Fortune, The Nation, The Democratic Digest, The Ensign, and the manual, How To Play Sneaky Tennis. Memorize page 2 of "Jokes Guaranteed to Lay Them in the Aisles." Anticipate that each Kennedy will ask you what you think of another Kennedy's (a) dress, (b) hairdo, (c) backhand, (d) latest achievement. You will find that "Terrific!" is a satisfactory answer. They won't listen to much detail.

WHAT TO EXPECT ON THE FOOTBALL FIELD

It's touch football, but it's murder. The only way I know of to get out of playing is not to come at all, or to come with a broken leg. If you don't have a broken leg and if you come, you will play; that is, you will if you don't want to take your supper in the kitchen, or if you want to talk to anyone for the rest of the weekend.

It is wise to know some football terms. The girls drop words like "button hook," "two on one," and "stop and go" with ease, as though they were sitting around the Harvard locker room — and I'm sure that when the weekend is over, you will feel that you have spent most of your time there. You will be wise not to suggest plays even though you were a star quarterback at school or college. The Kennedys have the play-calling department sewed up and all of them have received A-plus in leadership. If you see one make a mistake here and there, keep still — but never stand still. Run madly on all plays even if you weren't lucky enough to be signaled out in a huddle to carry out a mysterious assignment.

Make a lot of noise and make out that you never had a better time in your life. Things will go smoother if you do. Don't overdo this, though. Don't make out that you're having altogether too much fun. If you do, you'll be accused of not taking the game seriously enough.

Look glum if your team doesn't score a touchdown and become gleeful when your team does. Don't criticize your teammates. (It's a team game.) And for goodness sake, don't harp on any error of the enemy, because the enemy will be made up of Kennedys, too, and the Kennedys don't like that sort of thing.

If you want to become popular, show raw guts. They like this. To show raw guts is not an easy thing to do, but it will help if you fall on your face after every play. It also looks good if you smash into the house going after a pass. That shows that you are really trying. They like to see you playing on a twisted ankle or shrugging off a hole in your best suit. Simple things like that will help your game enormously. I know that it sounds incredible and that they might take the game a little seriously, but it's true; and, Oh yes! Don't be too good. Let Jack run around you every so often. It will be tough to fake, but it is a wise thing to try.

Don't, under any circumstances, let Ethel fool you. Never treat her either as pregnant or as a woman. Her husband has spent all of his spare time developing her change of pace, her timing on reverses, her endurance, and so forth, and she will make you look silly. My best advice to you is not to come at all; or if you do, rest your broken leg on a railing and cheer wildly for Bobby's team.

The comparison of Robert to Jack is similar to a comparison of Jack to Joe Junior. They excel in different fields. Still untried in politics is Edward, who is said to be a better orator with a more appealing stage presence than his brothers and these characteristics add up to a vote-getting ability. The girls are all as world-minded, as well traveled and as well informed as their brothers. They are outdistanced and overshadowed only because of their sex. Rose Fitzgerald Kennedy has one of the sharpest and keenest political minds in Massachusetts, as most elected and appointed public officials in the state well know.

None of the Kennedy children has shown the slightest inclination to follow in the footsteps of their father. Kennedy's office staff hoped fervently that Edward might show some interest and be trained to take over, but the hope is fading. He is still in the Kennedy stable, champing at the bit, waiting impatiently to get into competition with his brothers.

Robert Kennedy first emerged as a national figure in January, 1951. He was twenty-five years old when he joined the staff of the Criminal Division of the Department of Justice and was assigned to investigate the affairs of several regional Collectors of Internal Revenue. Two of them went to jail. It was not difficult for Robert to find a berth in Washington. His brother was then a Congressman and his father was serving on the Hoover Commission. The name "Kennedy" opened doors for him without the intercession of either. This was his first public service job and he acquitted himself well.

In 1953, he was appointed assistant counsel to Francis D. Flanagan, then chief counsel to the late Senator Joseph McCarthy's investigating committee. With McCarthy and Flanagan, he conducted the controversial hearings on how much strategic material was being shipped to Red China by the Western allies during the Korean War. Flanagan, however, was soon moved upstairs to the full government operations committee and he was replaced by Roy Cohn, a brilliant young lawyer about Robert Kennedy's age.

It was very quickly clear that Cohn and Kennedy could not get along together. They clashed frequently. McCarthy supported Cohn, and Kennedy quit in August, 1953, to become a staff assistant to his father on the Hoover Commission, studying the efficiency of the executive branch of the government. The Democratic members of the McCarthy subcommittee had already walked out on it. When the Democratic members returned to it in February, 1954, Robert Kennedy returned with them, this time at the request of Senator John L. McClellan of Arkansas. Kennedy's function was to advise and assist only the Democrats on the committee. Cohn remained as adviser to Senator McCarthy and the Republicans.

The feud between Kennedy and Cohn erupted again almost immediately. Both were quick-witted and sharp-tongued. Each was determined, insistent and quick to anger. The Army-McCarthy hearings began in February and dragged on into the spring. Throughout all of it the two were always at swords' points. In the beginning most of this was backstage and behind the scenes. Cohn, a chief counsel to the subcommittee, was in command. Kennedy did not like the way he handled the investigation and said so to Cohn and others.

The Army-McCarthy hearings were televised. A close friend of Roy Cohn and of Senator McCarthy was Private David G. Schine. Testimony at the hearings had indicated that Senator McCarthy had tried to get preferential treatment for Schine in the Army, possibly a commission and an assignment which would permit him to get to Washington and New York frequently.

The Army, it appeared from the testimony, would make no concessions for Schine. He could not be favored through political influence. Secretary of the Army Robert T. Stevens and Army Counselor John G. Adams had testified that pressure had been brought to bear upon them on behalf of Schine, a former subcommittee consultant and assistant to Cohn.

It was McCarthy's contention that the Army was holding Schine as a hostage to deter him from investigating Communism in the Army. In a cross fire of questions there was considerable merriment among the spectators when Democratic members referred to Schine's loneliness for his girl friend.

This resulted in a Cohn-Kennedy verbal clash. Their hot words brought from Chairman Mundt a warning that the feud must end. All of the committee members were basking in the limelight of television. Viewers had become fans and the two young lawyers were attracting the admiration of many.

The highlights of the weeks of TV hearings were Senator McClellan's cross-examination of Cohn on his and McCarthy's charges against Army Secretary Stevens, and Senator Jackson's quizzing of David Schine on a psychological warfare pamphlet he had written for the State Department; viewers rated them as superior entertainment.

Early in 1954, Robert Kennedy undertook an investigation into the Pentagon's procurement contracts and brought about the convictions of six persons for defrauding the government. It was here that his interest was first aroused in the whole field of labor-management relations and their effect upon government. It would be two years before he would be able to get back to it.

In January, 1955, the Democrats took over control of Congress and Kennedy became chief counsel of the subcommittee, succeeding Roy Cohn.

From 1954 to 1956, the subcommittee under Kennedy's direction pried into conflict-of-interest cases that ended the careers of Harold Talbott, Secretary of the Air Force, Hugh Cross, head of the Interstate Commerce Commission, and Robert Ross, Assistant Secretary of Defense.

ᵉᶳ 16 ᶳᵉ

THE MISSING LINK, the unanswered question, the unfinished story, piques the curiosity and intrigues the interest of Robert Kennedy. He has a bird-dog instinct for sniffing out a trail even when the quarry appears to have no relationship whatever to the object of the chase. If an answer to a question in an investigation is obscure and leads away from it, he cannot be satisfied until he clears it up.

An answer to a question in an Air Force investigation, for example, referred indirectly to the Interstate Commerce Commission. An action taken there would appear to be insignificant and of no compelling importance, but Robert Kennedy could not resist wondering: "Why?" Nor could he rest until he learned the reason. This originally led to an investigation of somebody or something in the Interstate Commerce Commission where another provocative question led to an investigation involving somebody or something in the Department of Defense.

That resulted in an examination of the Pentagon's procurement contracts; there Bob Kennedy's compulsion to expose the hidden or lay bare the secret caused researchers and investigators to reach into strange and unexpected places. A chemist and his wife in a town in New Jersey, a clothing manufacturer from Chicago, a former member of the Quartermaster Corps, among others, were brought to Washington to appear before the Senate investigating committee.

Chairman John S. McClellan, the members of his committee, and Counsel Kennedy questioned them. Some were casual and informative; some were cautious and shifty; some were indignant. The attractive housewife complained that Carmine Bellino, Kennedy's chief investigator, figuratively "twisted her arm" to make her talk. She protested that she was given promises of immunity for her husband — assured that he would be kept out of the subcommittee's investigation.

The questions grew sharper, more incisive, and narrowed down the area of truth. She acknowledged that she accepted gifts of clothing from two garment manufacturers while she was working for the government. Her brother-in-law, sitting beside her, handed her a note. She read it. Kennedy demanded that she read aloud the note she had just received. She refused. Chairman McClellan took over and insisted under threat of penalty. She read the note. It said: "You screwball."

Her brother-in-law was called upon to explain. He said he thought she was unnecessarily volunteering information to McClellan and Kennedy. There appeared to be contradictions in her testimony. She acknowledged that she told certain things to both Kennedy and Bellino, and when they had completed their investigation they came back to her and told her that most of her answers, when they first questioned her, were untrue. She became exasperated and addressing the committee said: "You wouldn't believe me now if I told you about the crack in the Liberty Bell."

The investigation ended. Six persons were brought into the courts along with the transcripts of the evidence before the Senate committee. They were found guilty of defrauding the government.

The case was over, but there were a number of unanswered questions still on the record — questions that these witnesses were not qualified to answer. They indicated something sour in the whole field of labor-management relations. Some of the contracts were stipulating to the United States government that uniforms delivered to various services had been manufactured in union shops, whereas they were, in fact, being made in non-union shops through payoffs to union leaders who were gangster-controlled.

This particular case might have been marked "closed," filed and forgotten, but Kennedy could not ignore the unanswered questions. From a single investigation that could have been dispatched in a couple of months sprouted another that took six months and spread into multiple investigations that would cover a couple of years and expose a pattern across the country of alliance between the underworld and some unions — among them the Teamster locals. The indications were that management either cooperated with union leaders, willingly, even enthusiastically, or that they were compelled by force to work hand in glove with them, with profit accruing to each.

There were indications, too, that the Senate committee would become a permanent investigative body — and it did — to clean up the whole situation and keep it clean. In any case, union leaders across the country and outside the clothing industry were becoming apprehensive. Successive investigations would take not months but years and inevitably there would be delays.

Early in 1955, for example, the subcommittee voted to ask for $192,000 to finance a search for graft, corruption, "infiltration" and waste in the government. Chairman McClellan announced that his committee had agreed unanimously that the first order of business would be to reopen their investigation of how the Army handled the case of Major Irving Peress and Pfc Marvin S. Belsky, a doctor of medicine. This unfinished business would take precedence over graft and corruption. It involved a survey of the Army's radar research center at Fort Monmouth, New Jersey. It was established that Communist infiltration there was confined to a few and was not widespread. It had already been cleaned up. The committee disposed of the case and went on to graft and corruption.

The program planned five years earlier by Supreme Court Justice William O. Douglas and Bob Kennedy had finally been cleared. The State Department had finally been successful in getting permission from Russia to permit both to visit the Middle East and behind the Iron Curtain. They decided to do so after the Supreme Court recessed and the Senate adjourned.

Justice Douglas is an experienced, inveterate world traveler. Because of that he was once characterized in Russia as an American spy. Robert Kennedy's background as a foreign correspondent did not make him popular there. Justice and Mrs. Douglas left early in June on the first lap of a three-month tour. Robert was to follow in late July and the three would meet in Teheran to enter southern Russia for an automobile and airplane trip, accompanied by an interpreter supplied by the Soviet government.

"The food was monotonous, but the journey was fascinating. You lose your appetite, but you see a lot," was the way Kennedy summed up the journey when it was over. An experienced photographer, he took many color and black and white shots, and hundreds of feet of motion picture film. The Russians changed the signals here and there, but all things considered he felt that they were treated with reasonable liberality.

They talked with the Prime Minister and the Shah in Iran. The Shah was interested in Kennedy's work as counsel for the Senate investigating committee and appeared to know what it was all about. He gave them some tips on what to look for among the villages along the shore of the Caspian Sea, revealed that he owned two hundred of them and was planning to give them back to the Iranian peasants.

They visited the fabulous lands of Marco Polo in central Asia, one of the least known areas on earth, traveling through country that stretches to the north of Iran, Afghanistan, Pakistan, India and Tibet, an historic area that had seen the conquering hordes of Alexander the Great, Jenghiz Khan and Tamerlane, generally identified on maps as Turkestan, which now comprises five Soviet republics.

Justice Douglas and Robert entered Russia by way of Iran on a boat that took them from Pahlevi to Baku on the Caspian Sea. Mrs. Douglas, not having a Russian visa, did not continue on the tour. They visited Krasnovodsk, a refinery city of 100,000 population, directly across the Caspian from Baku, and they were flown 345 miles farther southeast to visit Ashkhabad, an oasis of 200,000 population near the border of northeast Iran. Ashkhabad, like Krasnovodsk, is a "closed to foreigners" city.

Passengers and crew (which included a woman ship's doctor) aboard the boat remained aloof. They kept to themselves, ate by themselves and the two travelers saw them only when they were about to depart. Kennedy was prepared for that with a supply of ball-point pens, with which the crew was delighted.

Many of the workers they saw in the provinces were better dressed, better looking and better mannered than those they were later to meet in Moscow. There seemed to be no explanation for this. The workers were laying pavement, sidewalks, sewerage pipe and doing construction work at airports. Douglas and Kennedy visited radio stations, state farms and engineering schools turning out more engineers than the United States — about a thousand a year, 65 per cent of them women. They talked with a judge about automobile accidents. "We don't have them," the judge said. "Our drivers are disciplined."

A man on the street stopped Kennedy. "Are you a democrat?" he asked. "Yes," Kennedy answered and then added, "What do you mean by a democrat?"

"A person who has fought against oppression and for the people," the Russian answered.

Kennedy and Douglas found no free press anywhere they went, but there were plenty of loud-speakers everywhere shrieking the party line. The only Americans the people they met seemed to know were Eisenhower, Senator Joseph McCarthy and Senator Lyndon Johnson.

In Baku, they learned that the walls have ears. They were informed that they were now on their own, and their Russian guides were withdrawn. Henceforth, they were told, they must look out for their own transportation and hotel accommodations. This was a sudden and unexpected switch in the official arrangement, which had been to provide them with guides until the tour was over.

Douglas and Kennedy discussed it in a bit louder-than-normal voices in their hotel room. They agreed that the guides in Baku must be mistaken and that the proper way to settle the question would be to call Khrushchev in Moscow. Their suspicions were confirmed; the room was bugged with hidden microphones, for before the long-distance call could be made there was a knock at the door and an official explained in English that arrangements had just been made with Moscow to have a special guide assigned to them. This guide worked magic. Passengers were bumped off planes to make way for them when tickets were required at the last minute. The two Americans were given front row seats in every theater.

In Krasnovodsk, an intensely hot oil-refining center, there were wells but no drinking water, which had to be ferried to the city from Baku. There were no modern buildings. In a big square of apartment houses, there was no modern plumbing; instead, the apartments faced a common outhouse in the center. The travelers could find no mosques, no churches of any kind — not even a Russian Orthodox church.

The trip was informative and instructive, but Kennedy and Douglas were glad to complete it. When Kennedy left Washington, he had weighed 160 pounds, just as he had when he played football at Harvard. When he reached the south of France to visit his mother and father on the way home, he weighed 143. The people in the areas he visited did not lack food, but he had found it unappetizing and monotonous and it had been all but impossible for him to drink the water.

"We took along pills to put in it," he said, "but it still tasted as though you had drunk from a swimming pool. The only way the Justice and I got water was by eating a watermelon a day. It saved our lives. We had a heavy schedule and the heat in some places was unbearable. At Bukhara it reached a hundred and forty-five degrees.

"We could take the food for three or four days, but then we got tired of dishes like lamb's ear, scrambled lamb's brain or passing the head of a lamb around so you could take a bite. You lost your taste for it very quickly."

Throughout the trip they found that the people were friendly but Russian officials cool and aloof. Douglas and Kennedy were surprised at being questioned so closely by the ordinary man or woman in the street. Russians were still interested in the thirty-year-old Sacco-Vanzetti case. They seemed to be outraged by it and were somewhat molified when Justice Douglas told them that the robbery had involved a workers' payroll.

The Russians also declared that they disliked segregation and the American treatment of Negroes, yet the two travelers found segregation even more pronounced in Russia than in the States. The government practiced it in the colonization of non-Russian provinces. European Russians in these areas enjoyed better educational and recreational facilities than the local population. One set of schools was maintained for the children of Russians and another for native children.

Robert returned to the now-permanent Senate investigating committee when Congress convened in 1956, and would share microphones and cameras with his brother Senator Jack, huddling and whispering as they sat side by side listening to testimony. There were two impending outside events, however, that would occupy their divided attention. The first was the marriage of their youngest sister, Jean, and the other the Democratic National Convention in Chicago, which would later be given the undivided attention of all of the Kennedys, mobilized behind Jack *in the event that his name would be presented* as a candidate for Vice-President — typical political phraseology, as there was little doubt of its happening.

The Kennedy boom was not spontaneous — he did not emerge suddenly as a savior or a threat on the political horizon. It had begun more than a year before the convention in the mild speculation of political writers, essayists and pundits. Adlai Stevenson had had a hand in it; if he had not originated it, he stimulated it.

In August, 1955, a year before the convention, "persons close to Adlai" were quoted as saying that Kennedy would not only be satisfactory to him, but that he was, in fact, his first choice.

"So seriously is Kennedy being considered as possible timber for the Democratic national slate," James G. Colbert wrote in the *Boston Post*, "that party leaders in the South have already been sounded out about him and have declared that the junior Senator from Massachusetts would be acceptable to them. Many Massachusetts Democrats who are not enthusiastic about Stevenson," he went on, "would be forced to revise their views if Kennedy were his running mate, in view of the political impact the Senator would have in his own state . . . Stevenson and Kennedy are far closer than is generally realized."

In November, James M. Burns, professor of political science at Williams College, announced himself as a candidate for delegate to the Democratic National Convention because, he said, he wanted it to represent a grass-roots movement for Kennedy. He had neither informed nor consulted Kennedy about it. This, of course, did not make the Senator unhappy.

By January, 1956, the opinions of some political writers and commentators were inclining toward a contest between Adlai Stevenson and Senator Estes Kefauver for President and Senator Kennedy and Mayor Wagner of New York for Vice-President. Some of this public speculation was vaguely haunting and reminiscent of the Alfred E. Smith campaign, but it was the first time in the country's history, perhaps, that the religious issue was faced squarely and intelligently with such a large measure of acknowledgment that there had been an amelioration of traditional prejudice.

"No Catholic ever has been nominated for Vice-President," wrote Paul Healy, "but the feeling among national politicians is that it will happen sooner or later as religious intolerance continues to diminish. After all, they point out, who ever thought Maine would elect Governor Edmund S. Muskie, a Catholic?" A few years later he might have added: "Who ever thought Connecticut would elect Governor Abraham Ribicoff, a Jew?"

In March, Kennedy's prospects had improved to such an extent that the public analysts and political thinkers were approving Kennedy with reservations while taking him apart. He would strengthen the ticket, but there were drawbacks. One Senator was reported to have cautioned Kennedy:

"Jack, if you vote against high rigid supports for basic farm crops, I don't see how I can back you for the vice-presidential nomination."

"If I allowed considerations of the vice-presidency to influence my vote," Kennedy answered, "I couldn't live with myself — nor with my constituents" — and voted against them.

The conversation, however, symbolized the growing movement to draft him for Vice-President. It showed that he was being considered seriously by top Democratic brass. Frankly, Kennedy was not seeking the vice-presidential nomination at that time. He was not sure that he wanted it. The top brass was inclined to persuade him to that course.

The feeling among them was that religion had ceased to be a prime mover in American political life. A religious protest vote would be negligible; a generally favorable vote would be highly significant. There was little doubt now that his name would be among those on a short list of the acceptable to be handed to Adlai Stevenson at the convention, and as it was known that Adlai already favored him, it appeared that he would be the choice of the convention.

Politics make strange bedfellows. There is friction in any organization, even at the precinct level in public affairs. There are clashes of ambitions, motives and personalities. As an elected public official climbs the ladder, the critics within his own organization multiply. It is impossible for him to please everyone. The ambitious are sometimes frustrated by the very successes they helped to create. If a candidate rejects advice, depends upon his own judgment and succeeds, the adviser is embarrassed. If he accepts the advice and succeeds, the adviser expects the highest reward.

Kennedy was achieving national attention. His popularity was phenomenal. Unexpectedly he experienced mild irritation along the solid front at home. At the Democratic primary in April, 1956, Massachusetts voters were surprised to discover that Congressman John W. McCormack of South Boston, the former Democratic leader in the United States House of Representatives, was a favorite son for President in a quiet write-in campaign.

Among the sponsors of this popularity poll was William H. Burke, chairman of the state's Democratic Committee, who did not approve of Stevenson and was quoted as saying that "the supporters of Adlai Stevenson ought to be listening to Alger Hiss." Kennedy considered this a reflection upon himself, Governor Dever of Massachusetts and all other Democratic leaders of the state who had announced their support of Stevenson.

Kennedy took on McCormack, characterized Burke as unfit to be chairman and demanded that he be replaced. He had felt that way for some time, long before the primary. It was the first time that Kennedy had interfered in state party matters. When he told Burke why, Burke became angry and blew up. Kennedy felt that the fireworks at the state primary was a result. The two were in complete disagreement thereafter as to who had said what at their private meeting.

Kennedy was evidently of the opinion that Burke was dominated by McCormack and John Fox, publisher of the *Boston Post*. The *Post* was a Democratic newspaper, only recently acquired by Fox. It had bolted Stevenson four years earlier to come out for Eisenhower, a disappointment to both Kennedy and Governor Paul Dever. The dispute did not hurt Kennedy — actually it enhanced his popularity among the Democrats of the state.

Late in May, the Kennedys took a short recess from politics when Jean, who was still working with Father James Keller and the Christophers, was married to Stephen Edward Smith, an executive in the New York transportation firm of Cleary Brothers, founded in 1870 by his grandfather. Edward was a graduate of Polytechnic Pre-

paratory Country Day School in Brooklyn and Georgetown University. He had served in the Air Force as a first
lieutenant. This was a quiet wedding in the chapel of St.
Patrick's Cathedral; this ceremony too was performed by
Francis Cardinal Spellman.

It was generally acknowledged early in June that Adlai
Stevenson would be the choice of the convention. Senator
Estes Kefauver had been eliminated in a bitter primary
battle in spite of the endorsement of former President
Harry S. Truman and his attack upon Stevenson. The only
remaining threat to Stevenson was Governor Averell Harriman of New York and in the opinion of the politically
experienced he could not make it. Truman stood by his
guns. He predicted that Stevenson could not carry more
than the nine states he won in 1952.

Meantime, the Kennedy-for-Vice-President boom had
been growing bigger, louder and clearer. Late in June, at
the Governors' Conference in Atlantic City, Abraham Ribicoff proposed a plan to Democratic governors there that
they work for and support a Stevenson-Kennedy ticket.
He said he was sure Kennedy would be receptive. When he
was asked by newspaper correspondents if Kennedy's religion would be an issue Ribicoff answered:

"Since 1928, the country has reached a deeper sense of
maturity. Politicians are unimaginative when religious factors come up, but the people vote for a man on the basis of
his character, personality and principles. I am for Senator
Kennedy because of what he stands for. His religion
doesn't enter into it. I think he would add strength to the

ticket. He has always had a strong appeal for the independent voter. He did so in a year when Eisenhower carried Massachusetts in a landslide. He would have a wide appeal because he is a middle-of-the-roader. Southerners would like his position on most matters."

As the convention approached, the Kennedys and Kennedys-in-law were mobilizing for action; they now added up to fourteen politicking adults, including husbands, wives, two still unmarried and eight non-voting children, a total of twenty-two with the prospect that the clan would grow to much larger proportions.

Senator Jack was now bedeviled by insurrections within his party back in Massachusetts. There was no doubt that the name of John W. McCormack would be presented to the convention as a favorite son candidate for President. Kennedy had no objection to this. He had objected strenuously to the continuation of William H. Burke of Hatfield in western Massachusetts as chairman of the state Democratic Committee. Although he was state chairman, Burke had not been elected to the post. He had withdrawn as a candidate for re-election.

Democratic politics in Boston have always been confusing, with, inevitably, an element of legerdermain present. Too often political figures are pulled like rabbits out of a hat and are held aloft, given full prominence, displayed before the multitudes and are accepted. The law specifies that the chairman must be an elected member of the committee — chosen from the ranks. Burke was not. He became chairman as a result of a long court battle to oust his predecessor, John C. Carr. Burke's term ran out during the course of the litigation and he assumed the authority — one of those things that can happen in Massachusetts. He could be replaced only by another election or another court fight.

The Democratic State Committee had never been a power in Massachusetts. It was an interesting and useful collection of puppets. It provided one or more characters to synchronize their lips with the words. If the words were wrong, the character or characters were roundly trounced; if right, they were praised.

It could not be compared to the Republican State Committee, which was administered intelligently and functioned properly — an effective and powerful party organization. Kennedy recognized the need for a similar Democratic organization in the state and there was a good deal of enthusiasm and support among responsible Boston politicians for reforming the Democratic State Committee.

State Senator John E. Powers, a prominent Boston Democratic leader, said approvingly: "I never knew Burke to take part in any Democratic issue. As chairman, he has never given any help or assistance to Democratic candidates. You can ask any member of the legislature and they'll tell you, 'We've got to get rid of Burke for the good of the party.' Burke has exploited the party for his own good. The Democrats of Massachusetts need a new look and Burke certainly doesn't supply it."

Kennedy felt that the job had to be done. He gave no consideration to the certain retaliation invited by sticking his neck out. Congressman McCormack and James Michael

Curley were close friends. Chairman Bill Burke was their boy. Kennedy had disappointed McCormack and alienated both Curley and Burke when he refused to sign the Curley pardon petition nine years earlier.

Curley, McCormack and Burke were adamantly opposed to the candidacy of Stevenson. They would have accepted either Kefauver or Harriman. In their opinion, Kennedy already had two strikes against him. When Kennedy demanded the resignation of Burke, Curley, then eighty-one years old, stepped quickly into the act. He called a press conference and made a statement which might have come right from the mouth of Skeffington in *The Last Hurrah*.

"I see in the papers," he said, "that Mr. Burke says Kennedy wanted to know how much it would cost to get me off the Democratic National Committee." This was based on a conversation Kennedy had with Burke in which Burke had explained that he could validate his chairmanship of the State Committee very easily. He could be elected chairman by the members of the committee. He went on to reason that he could also be elected a National Committeeman in the same manner. Kennedy reminded him that this could not be done inasmuch as Curley had already been elected National Committeeman. "I wouldn't have any objection to you or anybody else succeeding Curley if he should retire," Kennedy said.

Thus was a simple conversation distorted so that it would suggest a proposed bribe.

"Well," Curley went on with his statement, "Kennedy

hasn't got enough money to buy me at any time. I never took any money from him or his whole family. Kennedy hasn't called me and if he did, I wouldn't speak to him.

"It's too damned bad," Curley went on "that he didn't count the vote in the Presidential primary for that fellow from 'The Last Hurrah.' What's his name? Skeffington. I'm supposed to be Skeffington and he got a hundred and sixty votes. Add that to my total and I would have topped the ticket."

This was Curley's whimsical view of the light vote in the Presidential primary. Privately he thought that he, and not McCormack, should have been the state's favorite son candidate for President, and the vote might have taught Kennedy not to dismiss him into retirement so lightly. The write-in favorite son victory of McCormack had rankled a number of Democrats. It had had to be stimulated by someone — probably Burke. McCormack's name had to be written correctly on the ballot. The write-in vote split the Democratic party in Massachusetts down the middle. Kennedy and Governor Paul Dever were for Stevenson: McCormack, Curley and Burke were opposed.

A favorite son nomination is an empty honor; it merely distinguishes a politician momentarily. A favorite son might have a vague hope that in the event of a deadlock at the convention political lightning might strike the favorites dead and leave the field to him. It happened to William Jennings Bryan after his Cross of Gold speech, but he could not make it in three tries. It is rarely mentioned, even in an obituary, when a favorite son dies. Will Rogers, the philosopher humorist, once proposed as such, made audiences from coast to coast laugh by discussing it as an odd singularity.

It is, however, a powerful political advantage at a convention. The state's delegates are pledged to him, and only he can release them at such time during the course of the convention as he sees fit. It clothes him with bargaining authority in the smoke-filled rooms. His price for relinquishing his delegates is patronage, the lifeblood of the politician — the appointments and their importance that will be awarded to him.

As matters stood then, McCormack would go to the convention as a favorite son.

❧ 17 ❧

ROBERT SARGENT SHRIVER and his wife Eunice knew their way around Chicago and Illinois politics. Sarge had a hand in the administration of Kennedy's Merchandise Mart there and was president of the city's Board of Education. Their home was a convenient and appropriate headquarters for the Kennedy women during the Democratic Convention. The men would stay downtown, handy to Convention Hall. Mrs. Shriver had two children then, two-year-old Bobby and eight-month-old Maria. They were farmed out, for the time being, at her parents' house on Cape Cod.

Mrs. Shriver was the first Kennedy to win a nomination at the convention. Even before the convention came to order, she and Mrs. Thomas Earl Keane, wife of a Chicago alderman, were appointed to be in charge of the entertainment committee. They proved to be a good team. Two weeks before the convention, Senator Kennedy's vice-presidential stock was moving up fast. Chairman John M.

Bailey of the Connecticut Democratic State Committee, like Governor Abraham Ribicoff, was a powerful and enthusiastic backer. As he saw it then, Kennedy's nomination could mean the difference between victory and defeat the following November. His canvass showed that almost every New England delegate to the convention was ready to support Kennedy.

The big question, the imponderable factor in Kennedy's candidacy, was and still is: Can a Catholic be elected President of the United States?

André Fontaine, the well-known New York reporter, correspondent, former associate editor of *Collier's*, currently a free-lance writer for magazines, posed the question on the eve of the convention this way:

"Senator, if you were running for President, we would want to have one question answered before deciding to vote for you. Conceivably there could be a situation in which the dictates of your church and the demands of your country would conflict. In such a case, where would your higher loyalty lie?"

"In the first place," Kennedy answered, "I can't think of any issue where such a conflict might arise. But suppose it did? Nobody in my church gives me orders. It doesn't work that way. I've been in Congress for ten years and it has never happened. People are afraid that Catholics take orders from a higher organization. They don't. Or at least I don't.

"Besides, I can't act as a private individual does; my responsibility is to my constituents and to the Constitution. So if it came to a conflict between the two, and not just a personal moral issue, I am bound to act for the interests of the many."

One of the arguments before and during the convention was that Kennedy would draw back into the Democratic party a phenomenal number of voters who had strayed into the Republican fold. The first great movement of Catholic Democrats into the opposition party came immediately after the defeat of Al Smith. Hundreds of thousands — the number never could be estimated — abandoned the party when the South turned thumbs down upon him in 1928, a move that they felt was due entirely to his religion.

A large and impressive number were drawn back into the party by Franklin D. Roosevelt, but a hard core of Catholics remained within the Republican party. Catholics generally in the Northeast are Democrats. The defection in Massachusetts helped to elect Saltonstall as Governor and Senator and Christian Herter as Governor. Catholics in the West and Midwest were inclined to be Republican even before Al Smith started campaigning.

There are fourteen northern states in which the Catholic vote is a sizable factor. How the Catholics in these states voted before 1940 never has been surveyed, but in that year President Roosevelt carried thirteen of the fourteen. In 1944, he carried eleven of them. In 1948, the number slipped to eight. In 1952, not a single one of these states was in the Democratic column. John M. Bailey argued that if Kennedy were nominated, he would bring all these states back into the Democratic column. They were not there in 1956. Eisenhower carried them.

As the convention approached, all of the Kennedys were in Chicago, well armed with such statistics and arguments. The six New England states with 104 votes were almost unanimously for Kennedy. The Kennedys and their womenfolk were diligently and tirelessly among the Senator's supporters—buttonholing delegates, chairmen of delegations and political leaders; persuasive evangelists petitioning for pledges and commitments. Significantly, during the time that they circulated among the delegates and political leaders, the religious question was rarely raised.

Elder statesmen and political veterans who had been present at the 1928 convention at which Al Smith was nominated, found an entirely different climate and atmosphere at this one; delegates from the South and West were not raising the religious issue — for the most part they ignored it. They were more concerned with Kennedy's position on price supports and segregation. The objection to Al Smith in 1928 had not been entirely on religious grounds. The major objections to Al Smith obviously were his association with Tammany Hall and his demand for repeal of the Prohibition amendment when the nation was not yet ready for it. Either that objection had been greatly exaggerated in 1928, or the country had matured to an astonishing degree in twenty-eight years. At any rate, the situation now was entirely different.

After circulating among delegations during the first day of the convention, John E. Powers, Massachusetts State Senate majority leader, concluded that Kennedy was almost certain to be the nominee for Vice-President and predicted that if he were, the Bay State election would be so strongly Democratic that the votes would have to be weighed instead of counted. There were confirming and contrary views. John Bailey estimated that Kennedy would add 132 electoral votes for the Democrats. Researcher Louis Bean found Kennedy unacceptable in farm states because he voted against rigid 90 per cent price supports, and observed that a Stevenson-Kennedy ticket would "put two dinner jackets" before the voters. In New York, Mayor Wagner said that issues affect Catholics and all others alike and characterized as a myth the idea that a Catholic would harm the party's cause.

The platform and resolutions adopted at that convention are now unimportant footnotes to history. The decisive moments came when Adlai Stevenson was nominated for the Presidency and Estes Kefauver for Vice-President; the most dramatic was the defeat of Kennedy by Kefauver. Governor Frank G. Clement of Tennessee opened the convention with his version of the customary denunciation of the Republican party and the administration. Mrs. Franklin D. Roosevelt, on the sidelines, endorsed Adlai Stevenson and suggested that leadership would best be given to younger men. Stevenson was then fifty-six; Kefauver, fifty-three. Ex-President Harry Truman declared for Governor Averell Harriman.

The favorite son candidates withdrew before the balloting: Warren Magnuson of Washington, and Representative John W. McCormack of Massachusetts. Senator John F. Kennedy narrated a film that he had made entitled "Pursuit of Happiness." It was well received in the convention hall. National Chairman Paul Butler called Kennedy to the platform when it was over and Kennedy was given an "ovation," an overworked word that somehow seems appropriate for a political demonstration. The Columbia Broadcasting Company refused to televise the film as part of the convention proceedings and was criticized on the air by Chairman Butler for it. Frank Stanton, president of the network, replied tersely: "Those who make the news cannot, in a free society, dictate to broadcasters, as part of a free press, to what extent, where and how they shall cover the news."

The name of Adlai Stevenson was formally presented to the convention on August 16 by Senator John F. Kennedy and the delegates went into the frenzied demonstration that was a commonplace for any candidate at any convention at the mere mention of his name. Kennedy described him as the man best qualified to lead the party and the nation, a great campaigner, an appealing figure.

"Our candidates will be up against two of the most skilled political campaigners in history [Eisenhower and Nixon], one who takes the high road and one who takes the low road." This brought loud and long applause, and Kennedy concluded by offering them "the man from Libertyville — and the next President — Adlai Stevenson." This brought the anticipated march around the hall by Stevenson supporters waving banners with inscriptions like: "We're madly for Adlai." It gave them a chance to relieve tensions, now that all awkward problems were temporarily solved. They had been up until early morning, after the session of the night before, trying desperately to sidestep a threatening fight over civil rights.

That evening Adlai Stevenson was nominated on the first ballot. Those who fell by the wayside were Averell Harriman, Lyndon B. Johnson, Stuart Symington, A. B. Chandler, James C. Davis, John S. Battle, George B. Timmerman, Jr. and Frank Lausche. Estes Kefauver had removed himself from consideration. He withdrew from the contest on July 31 after Stevenson had won at the California primaries.

The following day, Stevenson was on an embarrassing spot. It is customary for the winning candidate to choose his running mate. Kennedy had been his aide and associate. Kefauver had removed himself from competition and to that extent had promoted and simplified his nomination. He got off the spot tactfully by relinquishing his traditional privilege and leaving it to the convention to pick a Vice-Presidential nominee. The delegates did so that evening in an unprecedented, suspenseful drama that kept them and a Trendex-measured forty million TV viewers tense and on edge until it was over and done.

The first roll call is in the nature of a trial run and an opportunity to dispose of favorite sons. It is rarely an accurate measure of strength. In this case it was. The delegates and the TV audience watched a calculator, as impersonal as a cash register, and saw Kennedy's total climb to 304 with all others strung out in an also-ran field.

On the second round, the first important break toward Kennedy came when Arkansas cast its twenty-six votes for him. On the first roll call the state had gone to Senator Albert Gore of Tennessee. In the meantime, the delegation had caucused and Kennedy won the entire delegation by half a vote because it was under the unit rule. He continued to pick up votes here and there among the states until Minnesota was reached. On the first ballot, Minnesota's total vote had gone to Senator Humphrey. Now its chairman called thirteen and a half for Kefauver and sixteen and a half for Humphrey.

The clerk droned on, calling the names of the states. Kennedy was ahead of Kefauver, climbing at a fast rate while Kefauver climbed slowly. Missouri switched to Kennedy, as did New Jersey; then South Carolina, Texas and Mississippi fell into his column. It was clear now that Kennedy's strength was coming from New England and the South. Kefauver, from border state Tennessee, had voted with the North on racial matters. The South was punishing him. Their delegates preferred an outspoken Yankee who might even yell "Hooray for the Supreme Court!" to a doubtful Southerner whom they considered a renegade.

Kennedy's total moved slowly up to 600, 620, 630. He was within a step of going over the top. Like all candidates for President and Vice-President, Kennedy had held himself personally aloof during the convention. He would not enter the amphitheater except as convention tradition prescribed. He would not circulate among delegations or political leaders outside the convention soliciting votes or their assistance. A candidate enters the hall only in the final minutes when victory or defeat impends, hoping for victory or ready to congratulate the victor.

While the roll was being called, Senator Kennedy was

in his room at the Stockyards Inn, stretched out on a bed, fully dressed except for his jacket, watching the screen of a television set. He was alone. His wife was with the rest of the Kennedys in a box at the amphitheater watching the live show. Kennedy was tired. He had not slept for three days. His brother Robert was on the convention floor, going from delegation to delegation, particularly among the Southern states.

When Texas was reached on the roll call, Kennedy saw his good friend Senator Lyndon B. Johnson, chairman of the delegation, finger the microphone and say: "Texas proudly casts its votes for the fighting sailor who wears the scars of battle and the next Vice-President of the United States, Senator Kennedy of Massachusetts."

At that moment in the Stockyards Inn, Sarge Shriver shoved open the door of Kennedy's room; he was already behind events even though he had only crossed the street from the convention hall. Sarge said, conversationally, "Charlie Potter [the vice-president of the Inn] has given us an air-conditioned suite."

Senator Kennedy hardly heard and was not concerned. He jumped out of bed, grabbed his coat, dashed out into the hall with Shriver following. This was it — Kennedy was within twenty votes of nomination. States were waving their banners, seeking recognition of the chair to change their votes. He knew anything could happen. The race would be decided within minutes. He would win or lose before he could cross the street.

A flying wedge of policemen met him in the corridor. Newspapermen, still and television cameramen had rushed over to the Inn, in certainty of his nomination. Camera bulbs were flashing. TV lights were being turned on, but there was little time for all that. Police pushed and shouldered the crowd aside and broke a path through to the elevator. They escorted Kennedy across the street, a victor, but he arrived a moment too late for the dramatic climax.

Tennessee had been waving its banner for recognition. Sam Rayburn and John McCormack were both on the platform. A delegate from Tennessee called up to McCormack pleading with him to recognize Tennessee. McCormack nodded, walked swiftly to the podium and whispered to Rayburn, who recognized the state.

Senator Gore announced that he had released the delegates in that state pledged to him and Tennessee cast its votes for Kefauver. Pennsylvania, California and Minnesota quickly switched to Kefauver. Kennedy, so close to victory, arrived to find that he had lost. An analysis later showed that he had been defeated by half a vote in a unit-rule delegation.

Kennedy walked up to the platform and smiled at the crowd. The spontaneous demonstration was as lusty and as noisy as it would have been if he had been the winner. They cheered and whistled for long minutes. When order was restored, he said:

"Ladies and gentlemen of this convention: I want to take this opportunity to express my appreciation to Democrats from all parts of the country, North and South, East and West, who have been so kind to me this afternoon. I think it proves as nothing else can prove what a strong and united party the Democratic party is. I hope the convention will make this nomination unanimous."

The delegates roared and cheered. Kennedy turned to leave the platform, but Speaker Sam Rayburn called him back and handed him the gavel. Kennedy returned to the stand, held the gavel suspended a moment and went on: "I move we suspend the rules and nominate Estes Kefauver by acclamation."

Rayburn stepped forward and instructed all in favor to say "Aye." The delegates chorused it and with the time-honored prerogative of a presiding officer, Rayburn lifted his shoulders lightly and said, "No noes." Rayburn returned to his seat. Kennedy left the platform as the band played "The Tennessee Waltz." Although defeated, he left showered with laurels.

Kennedy had proved something to skeptics, doubting Thomases and unbelievers within his own religious faith, and he made a favorable impression. His experience indicated, at least, although it could not prove, that a Catholic does have a chance to be elected President of the United States and may have hastened the dawn of a new political era. He was not defeated because of his religion as so many political prophets had predicted. It was clear to any observer that the delegates had looked at his boyish face and tousled head thinking, "He's great, but he's young, only thirty-nine and he's got plenty of time."

The South cast the bulk of its vote — 288½ — for a Damyankee Catholic, a surprising action for delegates from a region so long considered by the North to be the source of racial and religious prejudice. Northern politicians must revise their opinions and change their sights. The Protestant South was willing to risk a Catholic on a national ticket, whereas heavily Catholic Pennsylvania was not.

There were other factors involved, it is true. Part of this Southern vote was a protest against the nomination of Kefauver because of his record. He had voted in favor of procedures that would have stripped them of their power; but as between a moderately liberal Senator from a border state and a not-so-conservative Yankee Catholic, they chose the Yankee. The hangover of the Smith campaign appeared to be cured.

John McCormack would have some explaining to do to his constituents and to the Democrats of Massachusetts. Immediately after the convention it would be all but impossible to make it clear that he was an innocent victim of circumstances. McCormack is anything but a vengeful person. He and Kennedy, like strong-minded, determined persons, can disagree and still be friends. Each has a deep respect for the other, as a good politician and a man of integrity.

McCormack had every reason to believe, as did most of the delegates and all of the television viewers, that Tennessee would switch to Kennedy. They could not know that long before the convention the delegation had voted to go to Kefauver if another Tennessee favorite son were not nominated.

It was sheer coincidence that McCormack was the message bearer, not the result of political intrigue. McCormack had accepted the inevitable. He had been in Kennedy's corner, fighting for him. It was not true, and as one national magazine said, that Kennedy's defeat could be attributed to the feud between Kennedy and McCormack.

The convention ended. The delegates streamed out. The amphitheater was already being darkened as Senator Kennedy walked across the street to the Stockyards Inn. He and Jacqueline had planned what they would do when the convention was over. He needed a rest and had arranged to take a plane next day straight from the airport to his father's house on the French Riviera. Jacqueline was six months pregnant and because of it not interested in a long overseas flight. She felt that she would be happier taking an air taxi to spend some time with her relatives in Newport.

Jack did not remain at the house in Val-sur-Mer very long. He was on a yacht on the Mediterranean when his father received word that Jacqueline had had a miscarriage. Jack did not learn of it until the boat reached port. He took the first plane home. The fact that he was not with Jacqueline when it happened made them, for the first time, subjects for gossip columnists who must have known, or at least should have known that there was nothing strange or unusual about their transient separation under the circumstances. Jack and Jacqueline were hurt badly enough without having their hurt further aggravated by public speculation designed to magnify a molehill into a mountain — one of the penalties exacted from those who must live in a political goldfish bowl.

The John F. Kennedys had been living in Virginia.

Both had been looking forward to the arrival of the baby. They had spent time, thought and money preparing a nursery. Now Jackie could not bear to look at it any longer, and they moved into a rented house in Washington.

Kennedy's speaking schedules for free time away from the Senate had always been crowded, but from the beginning of the Stevenson-Kefauver campaign immediately after the convention it became utterly impossible for him to take on even a small fraction of the speaking dates proposed for him. The Democratic National Committee was snowed under. He was in demand everywhere. As early as September 10, a tour around the country had been arranged for him.

He would be airborne for a full month: to Hartford to meet Adlai Stevenson on his first swing into New England; back to Washington next day to attend to Senate affairs; to Los Angeles to speak to the United Steel Workers; back to Hartford, to Lowell, Pittsburgh, Springfield, Boston, New Orleans, Grand Rapids, Detroit, Toledo, various cities in Virginia. In the meantime, he had his own personal mail problem. There were sacks of it in his offices in Washington and Boston. An analysis of it established that he not only had the women's vote, but the teen-age and small-fry vote. "All my family is Republican, but I stayed with you all the time, and when I get old enough, I'll vote for you," an eleven-year-old Montana girl wrote. A nine-year-old boy in Illinois wrote: "I ran out of the room when you lost." Every Democratic leader in every state seemed to be working out a schedule for

Kennedy. Former Senator J. Howard McGrath, acting campaign manager for Estes Kefauver in Rhode Island, rated him the Number Three Campaigner for the Democrats.

He was a confident speaker, versatile and effective on television, radio or in person, but careful in his use of words. He made no rash or absurd predictions. He intended that voters should get the impression that he was sure of victory, persuading them to the belief without ever actually saying so. He would say, for example, that "the professional pessimists, the pollsters and the Republicans won't believe that Adlai Stevenson is going to win," which, of course, was the truth. The implication was that Stevenson must win; he would then continue with other truths like: "The G.O.P. claims that it is the party of the future and the party of peace, progress and prosperity. The future belongs to the strong, not the weak. It belongs to the courageous, not the complacent. We are the party of the future — and the future belongs to us."

An examination of his speeches reveals that they are so contrived that it would be difficult, if not impossible, to lift sentences and paragraphs out of context to give them a different meaning or to confront him later with exaggerations or inconsistencies. This is a trick of writing and oral delivery that requires consummate skill. In this particular, at least, some of them are classics. They are, moreover, adjustable, so that a few quick changes even during delivery would make them fit any situation, yet the built-in flexibility of the design could not impair their effectiveness. They have been used by teachers of elocution and in public speaking classes as illustrations of technique and examples to follow.

Kennedy is hardly a speaker to heckle. He is too quick-witted and his response is immediate and concise, neither insulting nor embarrassing, usually made with grinning good-nature. Arthur Larson, Director of the United States Information Agency, on one occasion suggested before a Women's National Press Club audience that Senator Kennedy become "a new Republican."

"One temptation to accept Mr. Larson's invitation to become a New Republican," Kennedy answered, "is the fact that I would be the first Senator in either party to do so."

Kennedy was disappointed twice during 1956. He lost the vice-presidential nomination by a hair and his candidate lost the election, yet Kennedy had won something invaluable by these defeats. He was one of the few losers in American history to emerge with greater stature and prestige than he had going into the campaign. Except for Estes Kefauver, he had traveled more, given more speeches and met more people than any other Senator. He had acquired a large measure of national admiration and respect, but the questions remain to be answered.

Can a Catholic be elected President of the United States? Can Kennedy be elected President of the United States? Can a Catholic be elected Vice-President of the United States? Would Adlai Stevenson have been elected President of the United States if Kennedy, instead of Kefauver, had been nominated for Vice-President? Did the fact that he had lost by such a close margin alienate Democrats in enough states to elect Eisenhower?

Kennedy was in a unique position when the Senate convened in January. He returned as one of the most widely known political figures in the country, next in importance and prestige to the two top men, Stevenson and Kefauver, and yet he held no title in the party, nor did he serve on any of the ranking committees in the Senate.

Although he had had eleven years' experience in Congress and as a junior Senator, he had not, until now, been given any of the assignments he sought in the Senate. The party was now in debt to him. He had asked for either the Appropriations Committee or the Foreign Affairs Committee, for which he was particularly qualified. Few Senators had seen more of the world than he, in the Navy and as a world traveler who went to the places and talked to the people who interested him. Even among those who were traveled, he had been to the same places more often and remained longer. It was in the nature of a hobby with him — an all-consuming interest.

He made a number of points in his memorandum to Senate Majority Leader Johnson: (1) Every Democratic Senator with more seniority than he already had an assignment to a major committee; (2) nearly all Democratic members of the Senate Foreign Relations Committee had equal or less seniority than he when they were assigned to that committee; five of eleven Democrats on that committee had equal or less seniority when they received their assignments; (3) he was the only Democrat who came into the Senate in January, 1953, who had not improved his committee assignments.

He advanced other arguments in the same vein that seemed to indicate he had been the Senate's whipping boy. Powerful arguments, however, are never as effective as political strategy. He wanted an appointment to Foreign Relations and got it, and he also was appointed to the Permanent Subcommittee on Investigations for which his brother Robert was counsel. Lyndon Johnson and Kennedy were close personal friends, and Kennedy's star was rising. Both parties begin planning the next election the day after the President takes office. Kennedy was out front, and might well be the candidate in 1960.

Kennedy returned to the Senate to share the limelight with his brother Robert while at the same time carrying out an almost superhuman schedule. He was named as chairman of a special Senate committee to pick the five most outstanding Senators in the nation's history, a result of his Pulitzer Prize book *Profiles in Courage*. He waded into a number of economic problems that affected New England, tackled the Interstate Commerce Commission on discriminatory freight rates for Boston and New England shippers and went to work on the White House and the Tariff Commission for protection of the region's textile industry.

The New England Senators Conference began to fight with the Office of Defense Mobilization over restrictions sought by foreign oil importers. He fought to salvage a federal flood insurance program that was cut out of the budget by the House and plugged for swift action on New England flood control projects.

John Kennedy had no need to learn how unhappy lies the head that wears a crown. He had had earlier lessons. Popularity begets criticism. Extremists on both sides, from ultra-conservatives to Communists, were sharpshooting at him. Isolationists ripped him apart for his views on the McCarran-Walter Immigration Act and criticized him for saying that American schoolchildren should be taught more about foreign affairs. The New York *Daily Worker* attacked him for being too moderate. Liberal publications were bitterly sarcastic because he agreed to include the late Senator Taft among the list of the five most outstanding Senators.

But honors too continued to flow his way. In June he was elected one of five Harvard alumni to serve on the Board of Overseers for six years. He had topped the entire field of candidates, polling 14,213 votes by alumni. It was the first time that a Catholic layman had been voted to the board. A year earlier he had received an honorary degree from Harvard.

In July, Senator Kennedy whipped up a storm that caused repercussions around the world. In a full-dress Senate speech he called upon the Administration to stop supporting France's Algerian war and to begin working for Algerian independence. As chairman of the Senate Foreign Relations Subcommittee on United Nations Affairs, he attacked what he characterized as the Administration's "head-in-the-sand policy," and he backed up his criticism and the chief point in his speech by introducing a resolution calling upon the President and the Secretary of State to place the influence of the United States behind efforts to bring about independence for Algeria.

The United States had been siding with its old ally, France, against Algeria's demands for complete independence. Kennedy said that the United States was failing to meet the challenge of imperialism as against independence in both Algeria and Poland and informed the Senate that he would soon make a speech on Poland's fight for independence. The French people were outraged by what he said and the French press generally scolded him by saying, in effect, that the French-Algerian situation was none of his business. Kennedy had an important French vote in Massachusetts to consider, but insisted that he must speak his mind in spite of it. When he had, there was not much repercussion among his French constituents.

The debate became a three-cornered affair, with Paris, Washington and Algiers participating. The French Minister to Algeria accused Kennedy of being "an ambitious parliamentarian" who fell for rebel propaganda, and characterized him as being among the old maids and Quakers in the United States. Kennedy answered him by saying that the Algerian situation resembled a deadly time bomb ticking toward another disaster to the free world. Secretary of State Dulles said that Algeria was primarily a French problem and that it was so complex that he would be very sorry to see it made ours. The Administration stuck to its policy.

Kennedy did not succeed in altering United States foreign policy, but the results of a Gallup poll released at about the same time showed that he was now the country's favorite Democrat in Number One position. The question was asked of Democrats: "Suppose the choice for the Democratic nomination in 1960 for President comes down to one between Senator Kefauver and Senator Kennedy, which of these two would you personally favor?"

In February, 1957, the vote was Kefauver, 49 per cent; Kennedy, 38 per cent; undecided, 13 per cent. In July, it was: Kennedy, 50 per cent; Kefauver, 37 per cent; undecided, 13 per cent.

In November, Jacqueline gave him a prize that topped all others — a daughter, weighing seven pounds and two ounces, who was baptized in St. Patrick's Cathedral, New York, where her parents had been married, and christened Caroline Bouvier Kennedy after Mrs. Kennedy's sister, Mrs. Caroline Canfield of New York.

✺ 18 ✺

THE KENNEDY BROTHERS, John F. and Robert, were associated in the public mind from the beginning of 1957, when the Senate Permanent Investigating Committee resumed its hearings on labor racketeering, begun during the previous session. The Senator was now a member of that committee. His brother sat beside him. Except for height and weight, they were look-alikes, familiar to nationwide television audiences.

Their temperaments and mannerisms were different. The Senator was silent, thoughtful, contemplative as he asked an occasional question of a witness. Robert was quick, brusque, a biting bulldog when aroused, determined to score his point in an examination, outspoken, often plainly irritated by some of the labor leaders who came before the committee as well as by their high-priced lawyers. Many of them resented being ordered around by a tart-tongued whippersnapper who looked young and fresh enough to be back on an Ivy League campus concerned with affairs like the senior prom.

Curiously enough, Robert Kennedy could get along better with some of the labor leaders than with their lawyers. He exchanged badinage and wisecracks with Frank Brewster and Dave Beck of the Teamsters Union, chatted so amiably with them during recesses that they sometimes forgot to guard their tongues. During one such corridor chin session when a "loan" of $270,000 to Dave Beck was in question, Brewster told Kennedy that he thought the loan had been recorded on the union books.

Kennedy slipped away quietly to a telephone in a hearing room, called the union bookkeeper in Seattle and established that no such loan had been recorded; then he called Brewster to the telephone to hear the bookkeeper confirm it. A few minutes later, when the hearing was resumed, Brewster testified that he knew of no such loan and thus drove another nail into the case against Dave Beck.

This was characteristic of Robert Kennedy. He was a demon for checking every statement, including the evidence uncovered by his own agents — and he had, perhaps, the most complete fact-finding organization ever known on Capitol Hill; fifty-five well-organized accountants and investigators, a well-oiled machine, hitting on all cylinders. Robert Kennedy's righthand man was Carmine Bellino, a skilled detective-accountant always in command when Kennedy was not directing the men personally. He and Kennedy did much of the sleuthing together and put the evidence that would bring labor leaders before the courts into the hands of Chairman Senator McClellan. Kennedy and Carmine were threatened verbally by tough characters both in Chicago and Washington and were often

upbraided in the corridors of the Capitol by witnesses before the committee.

They followed leads from city to city and state to state,
questioning, digging, telephoning, knocking on doors, ringing bells, isolating suspects and interviewing them. Attorney Kennedy always characterized these investigations,
including the big ones, as unromantic drudgery.

Suspect labor leaders came to have a covert respect for
him, revealed only when they were trapped. James R.
Hoffa, for example, was a tough-talking, hard-boiled chief
of a Midwestern union. Senator McClellan, Kennedy and
the FBI worked together and in secret to ensnare him. He
was caught with documents stolen from the committee
and as a result was indicted. He was brought into a Washington court at midnight on March 13, 1957. Kennedy
was there waiting for him.

Hoffa smiled at Kennedy genially and quipped: "I can
do twenty-seven push-ups. How many can you do, Bob?"

Kennedy responded with a grin, "I can do fifty."

Kennedy's friends knew he could do more than sixty.

The lawyer and the Senator were not in competition
for headlines. They shared them. Once when Senator Mc-
Clellan was summoned hastily from the room as a witness
was coming forward to be sworn, Senator Kennedy,
obviously lost in thought, did not realize that he had suddenly become acting chairman of the committee. A nationwide television audience was amused to observe Attorney Kennedy poke Senator Kennedy in the ribs, saw
him look up suddenly and rise to have the witness sworn.

Throughout 1957 and 1958, Robert was the bane of

all union leaders with something to hide. He went on with an investigation of the then four-year-old Kohler plumbing fixtures strike in Wisconsin. During the recess of 1958, the brothers came back to Massachusetts, John F. as a candidate for re-election to the United States Senate and Robert as his campaign manager. Political leaders throughout the country prepared to watch that campaign.

Early in 1958, John F. Kennedy posed a problem that frustrated the Republican party in Massachusetts. Long before the Republican state convention, party leaders were certain that Kennedy could not be defeated. For a time they contemplated letting the Republican nomination go by default by naming no candidate for the United States Senate. It was too difficult to find one. Then they considered nominating a token candidate, one who would spend no money and make no fight. Ultimately they decided to offer a sacrificial goat, a well-known candidate of considerable prestige in the Republican party, Charles Gibbons, minority leader of the State House of Representatives. He would make a determined fight, and in the almost probable event of defeat, he would be politically rewarded.

One of the chief difficulties the Republicans faced was that Kennedy would get not only the Democratic vote, but a sizable share of the Republican vote. His popularity crossed party lines. The organization of the New England Council of Senators benefited all of them politically. It was no secret that Kennedy and Saltonstall got along very well together. They sought legislation jointly, agreed upon the nature and language in bills. They signed jointly and the news was released under their names. Massachusetts, and for that matter, all of New England approved of this kind of cooperation. The average voter, whether Democratic or Republican, never had it so good, and it would take considerable persuasion to change his mind. If he asked for the assistance of one, he got it from both.

Massachusetts voters in 1958 were sure they were voting for a Senator who would be a candidate for President. His popularity had been gathering momentum and growing since the convention of two years earlier. The question, Can a Catholic be nominated and elected President of the United States? had been receding in importance.

Shortly before Christmas, in 1957, Kennedy was interviewed on NBC in the council chamber of Boston's Old State House, as a member of the Bostonian Society which maintains it, by Martin Agronsky, who raised some interesting questions.

He reminded listeners that a million dollars had been settled on the Senator at the age of nine, acknowledged that he had discharged a duty to his country during World War II and suggested that as he was already the author of a best-seller he might have pursued a literary instead of a political career and inquired why a man so well fixed did not live a life of ease. Kennedy answered that he thought the hardest work a man could do was to live a life of complete leisure.

"I feel that being a Senator is the most interesting job in the country. If I were in a law office, I would be working on someone's will or brief, or for a corporation advancing some private interest. In politics, all of us have views on what ought to be done and in Congress, at least, you have an opportunity to implement some of the things you feel strongly about."

"Senator McCarthy is gone," Agronsky said, "and there are many people who feel — and some who have said — I'm sure you have heard the crack, making a play on the title of your book, that you should have shown a little less profile and a little more courage in connection with the censure of McCarthy. It is only fair to point out that you were in the hospital at that time and could not have voted. Would you, or would you not, have voted to censure Senator McCarthy?"

"I have pointed out on many occasions," Kennedy said, "that I had been away from the Senate for nine months when that came up. I was not then a member of the jury. I would have been perfectly prepared if it came up in the summer of 1954; but it did not come up while I was in the Senate and I was not equipped for it when it did come up. It came up only three or four weeks after I was in the hospital. I have said since then, based on the evidence presented and upon Senator McCarthy's transgressions of the rules of the Senate that I thought the censure was a reasonable action. I don't know what more I can say about it."

"Could your religion conceivably ever influence your conduct or judgment as a Senator, as a member of the House or as President of the United States? I raise the question. I feel it an unpleasant one —"

"I don't think it is unpleasant at all," Kennedy interrupted. "Of course your religion has an effect upon all of your actions, I would hope. If action is based on any moral or ethical plane, naturally your religious convictions influence you. Whether they do or not, or whether we meet the standard we would like to meet is another thing; but of course it does have some influence."

"Well," Agronsky continued, "let us discuss it then in the political sense. There are many who feel justifiably or unjustifiably that were a Catholic to be in the White House, he might be influenced, let us say, by directions or opinions or inclinations of the Vatican. How would you respond to that?"

"Obviously, Martin," Kennedy answered, "there is nothing the Pope — when you say the Vatican, I assume you mean the Pope — could say that would have any effect upon my Constitutional obligations. I swore an oath to defend the Constitution when I went into the Navy and I've taken it four times since in my election to Congress. It's the same oath, I believe, as the President takes; in effect, its essence is the same.

"The Pope speaks as the head of the Catholic Church. My faith is a personal matter and it doesn't seem to be conceivable, in fact it is impossible, that my obligation as one sworn to defend and uphold the Constitution could be changed in any manner by anything the Pope could say or do. What church I go to on Sunday, what dogma of the Catholic Church I believe in is my business and whatever faith any other American has is his business. It does not in any way involve public questions or policy or as the Constitution defines the responsibilities of the President, Senator or member of the Armed Forces."

"The country has changed considerably since 1928," Agronsky suggested.

"I hope I have been specific about it," Kennedy went on. "It is the obligation of a public servant to defend the Constitution. It is *the* obligation. What prayers he says, whether he goes to church on Sunday or fasts during Lent are his affairs. I hope that everyone has some religious conviction. If they don't, their rights are also protected by the Constitution. Merely because the Catholic Church is an international church, in the same sense that all religions are, and covers more than state boundaries, there is no reason why that personal faith in any way limits a person's obligation to perform his Constitutional duties.

"Canada has had three Catholic Prime Ministers. Here in the United States, for two-fifths of the time that this country has been in existence, we have had a Roman Catholic head of the Supreme Court which, after all, does have extraordinary powers in interpreting the Constitution. I really do not see why Catholics are not as completely equipped to meet their Constitutional obligations as anyone else."

"I think that's a specific answer," Agronsky said. "I asked the question because it will be raised."

"It will be if a Catholic is a candidate. I am not a candidate. I am running for the United States Senate in Massachusetts in 1958. These questions are for people who think it is fitting to discuss them."

"I don't know whether I should let that 'you're not a candidate' go by, but I am tempted to. Everyone would be inclined to say that you'd accept the offer, but I'm not going to ask you. I wonder if you could tell me, to clear up this issue — and I think you have been specific — Al

Smith said in 1928, 'I believe in absolute separation of Church and State.' Would you echo that?"

"I think it's unnecessary to echo it, but I will echo it. There are a number of countries where there is no separation of Church and State. There isn't in England. In certain countries where the Catholics are dominant, the position of Catholics in relation to the state is a very influential one; but in our country the whole system is based upon a separation of Church and State and I am wholeheartedly in favor of it."

"Tell me," Agronsky went on, "do you think that our country has changed since 1928 in relation to a matter like religious bias and bigotry?"

"I think there are evidences of a greater comprehension of the obligations which the citizens have, whatever their religious faith may be. I remember reading about the objection raised to the seating of Senator Smoot because he was a Mormon. Today that question never would come up. There has been an evolutionary development in the United States. Whether the question would be raised again if a Catholic should become a candidate for President, I don't know."

"You don't feel that the country might have become more tolerant, perhaps more mature, more sophisticated? Do you see any change in that direction?"

"I think there is greater knowledge," Kennedy answered. "I think that many of the things said about Smith were based upon complete ignorance. I think there is wider knowledge now of the doctrine of the Catholic Church which would have permitted Al Smith, if he had been elected, to fulfill the obligations of the office. There is greater understanding. Whether there is complete understanding or not, I don't know. I suppose we'll have to wait until the time comes. It might be raised again, but I don't know."

"I'm sure it will be," Agronsky said.

✥ 19 ✥

PUBLIC INTEREST in a defeated candidate for any office normally wanes after a convention. He had his chance and failed. Sustained public interest in a vice-presidential candidate's runner-up at a political convention is unheard of, or at least rare.

What would have happened if Kennedy had been the nominee? Would Stevenson have been elected? If the test had been made and Adlai Stevenson lost, the question: "Can a Catholic be elected President of the United States?" would possibly have been held to be answered. Kennedy might have been charged with the responsibility for Stevenson's defeat and would not now be in the foreground as a candidate for the Presidency. If Adlai had won, respect for the Catholic vote might have benefited Catholic states, yet Kennedy might not have been contemplated as a candidate for President. No doubt Adlai would have been a candidate for re-election to the Presidency with Kennedy as his running mate.

Thirty-eight and a half votes at an exciting and suspenseful convention created the situation that the Democratic party and the voters of the nation now face. The big question remains unresolved. Polls and surveys, newspaper and private, indicate a growing national disposition for a showdown.

As a result of Kennedy's near-victory, his campaign for re-election to the Senate in 1958 assumed an unusual importance. There was never any question about the outcome. That was a foregone conclusion. Republicans acknowledged it privately and all but conceded the election to him.

Republicans and Kennedy's enemies among the Democrats — inevitably, he had a few — surreptitiously ascribed this certain triumph to the expenditure of Kennedy money. They were wrong, Kennedy could have gone to the South Seas for the duration of the campaign and still have been elected, but the size of the vote that he was to get had now become important as a demonstration to the rest of the country of what his home state thought of him. It was clear that he would be nominated by acclamation at the state convention.

No Republican wanted to face him. Charles Gibbons, who had been picked to oppose him, was unhappy about it. He had been persuaded to do so "for the good of the party" and regretted that he had consented.

When the Republican convention convened in Worcester in June, 1958, Gibbons took the platform to say: "It does not become me to be a sacrificial goat. I will not be a candidate for United States Senator. It was my original intention to seek the nomination for Governor of Massachusetts. I intend to do that regardless of the action of this convention. I will enter the primaries to contest for the nomination against the choice of this convention."

George Fingold, the nominee, died before election day. Republican party leaders agreed upon Gibbons as their candidate for Governor. Vincent J. Celeste, a little-known East Boston attorney, had been chosen by the convention to face Senator John F. Kennedy. Celeste had a delicious sense of humor. During the campaign he made the grinning observation that he felt as if he were running for the United States Senate on five gallons of gas. Foster Furcolo was picked by the Democratic convention as the candidate for Governor against Gibbons. Kennedy, as expected, was nominated by acclamation.

The appearance of these two names, Vincent J. Celeste for United States Senator and Foster Furculo for Governor, marked the completion of a cycle and the end of an era. The curtain was falling on a final tableau that might be titled "The Vanishing Boston Irish," a vivid grouping of elderly, worn-out political leaders, including the stooped, wrinkled and emaciated king of them all, James Michael Curley, silent and motionless in appropriate postures — the last of the Mohicans.

The prophecy concerning the limitation of the size of families made by William Cardinal O'Connell so often a generation earlier was now fulfilled: The Boston Irish had aped the Brahmins and the bluebloods too closely, and unlike Kennedy, they had small families. Now, they had the money, but not the votes. The second great tidal wave of immigration from 1896 to 1906 had caught up with them and washed over them. These immigrants had come first from Italy and then from Poland and Lithuania.

The number of Italian-American voters throughout the state, and particularly within the metropolitan district, had become impressive enough in 1958 to decide a close election. Boston's Italian-descent voters are usually Democrats. The rest of the state is divided. Celeste's "five gallon" campaign dramatized the Kennedy money.

Republican speakers picked it up, and emphasized it, for lack of a better issue. Critics were to keep it alive long after the campaign. Joseph P. Kennedy was pictured as a millionaire sitting in a room at the Ritz-Carlton, surrounded by moneybags, handing it out to all comers and buying up every political leader in the State.

A friendly reporter who kept in touch with Curley dropped by his house and during the course of a conversation brought up the subject of the money and how it was reported to be spent. Curley contemplated the question like a politician and for the moment ignored his cold war with the Kennedys. "Is there any voter, man or woman, anywhere in the country," he asked, "who doesn't know and acknowledge that money must be spent by and for every candidate for public office from City Alderman up to President of the United States?

"How far would any candidate get if he merely announced that he intended to run for an office and would not spend a penny out of his own pocket or permit his friends to spend any of their money to help elect him? It may have happened here and there in rare instances where a candidate running for re-election was so popular that it would be futile to enter the lists against him.

"Politics is not for the poverty-stricken," he went on. "A candidate without funds cannot even reach an audience. He may stand on a street corner — common practice before radio and television — and try to assemble an audience by giving a speech. A handful of the curious might stop a moment to look and listen, shake their heads and continue on, characterizing him as a crackpot. The voters would be home watching their television screens either interested in what a candidate had to say or condemning them for interrupting more interesting programs. Thirty-five or forty years ago," he reminisced, "the bankrupt candidate was commonplace on street corners, in parks and public halls for weeks before primaries and elections. Even though his opposition was equally impoverished, he was inevitably fighting the rich, entrenched wealth and 'The Interests.' It was a standard pattern. I know. I used it very successfully myself.

"The candidate was inevitably the son of poor but honest parents. He had to struggle for a livelihood since early childhood. He was a bootblack, a newsboy or both. He attended school fitfully. One or both of his parents were temporarily or permanently invalids. Despite poverty and all of these hardships, he managed to complete courses in grammar or high school or both. Otherwise he was self-educated. He would never admit that he was pitifully equipped for public service; but he was game.

"That was a day when you could buy votes across the

table in almost any ward boss's shop. You made a down payment before election and paid the balance C. O. D. on the day after election. If the returns showed that you lost the ward, you lost your down payment and could do nothing about it. If the returns showed that you carried the ward, that was one bill you had to pay or go to jail.

"If you won the election and welshed on the payment, you'd be warned that you would be charged with attempted bribery and confronted by witnesses who saw you offer the money to the ward boss before election, and the ward boss had righteously rejected it and threw you out of his office.

"That was a day, too, when precinct captains could herd scores of voters into barrooms throughout the day and buy a vote for a drink. That was cured by legislation, but the hangover remains. In spite of the fact that it would be absurd today for any candidate to buy a vote for a drink, it still remains impossible to buy an alcoholic beverage in any package store, bar, tavern, dining room or hotel in the city, an inconvenience for residents and tourists.

"The fact is: In that day, the votes went to the richer of two poor but honest candidates.

"They began to fade from the scene in the early twenties. There were two causes: The results of compulsory school attendance were becoming apparent. More and more children were being graduated from elementary schools. Enrollments in high schools and colleges had been swelling. The sudden development and wildfire popularity of radio changed political techniques overnight. An illiterate sympathy pleader in a political race was left at the post. At the same time, the old fashioned ward boss was losing his grip and going into decline. His tricks and deceptions would no longer work. He found it more difficult to cajole and persuade. The average voter was better educated and informed. Men and women who never would contemplate attending a national convention listened for days to the monotonous refrain in 1924 'Alabama casts twenty-four votes for Oscar W. Underwood.'

"The big political revolution would come five years later. Prohibition had spawned the bootlegger, the gangster, gunman and particularly the racketeer, who moved in later upon legitimate business and still remains to plague us. The stock market crash shocked the nation. Everybody, including the poor but honest, had been playing the market. The depression pulled the rug from under those who felt so secure, and a whole population got a political education the hard way very quickly.

"Most of the professional politicians in the big cities across the country floundered and were washed away. They couldn't help themselves, let alone the voters in their districts. Some of us managed to survive, Tom Pendergast in Kansas City, Frank Hague in Jersey City, Ed Kelly and a handful of others, including myself. Prohibition was repealed. Roosevelt proclaimed the New Deal and brought a swarm of intellectuals into prominence. The old line politician swallowed them hard. He had no choice.

"Today the voters can't be fooled. They can't be deceived. They can't be duped. At all ages they've been through too much. They are world-minded, national-

minded and civic-minded. The voting majority is now too
well educated, too aware of what is going on around them
to be misled by an inept politician. Both politics and crime
have become big business, although they are not necessarily
related.

"Politics has become a profession and any young man
who yearns to enter it had better contemplate it as such.
He must train for it and prepare for it. He must be a college graduate. It is no longer a refuge for a misfit who
asks the public to hire him because he is self-educated and
obviously out of a job. Making that plea, he would have to
be a veteran, and if he were, voters would ask: 'What's
the matter with him? Why didn't he complete his education and go to college on the GI Bill?' He couldn't even
carry his own precinct.

"Today's candidate for almost any office must have
money or friends who are willing to invest in him by way
of contributions — preferably both.

"Today you cannot buy votes across the table under
any arrangement," Curley went on. "No leader or elected
public official would bargain or sell. If he did he would be
delivering himself into the hands of the purchaser. Politicians are familiar with the laws governing elections and the
rules established for conventions. You can negotiate for
votes at a convention, where no money is involved, but
candidates are allergic to scandals associated with elections.

"Under today's system, you buy the whole election in a
package deal. The candidate with the most money hires the
biggest and best advertising agency to contract for television and radio time, space in newspapers and magazines,

billboards and spectaculars, posters, placards, direct mail, telephone salesmen and solicitors talking to voters, the persuaders using the 'hard sell' or the 'two call soft sell.' They furnish sound trucks. They have idea men who come up with slogans, buttons, and gimmicks, and if you want the full treatment, they'll take weekly polls. For doing all this, they get fifteen per cent of what they spend, but from the media.

"This is backed up by your own organization, the contributors and workers who flock to you, convinced by your spectacular splurge that you can't lose. They will man your headquarters in every ward in the city, or every city or town in the state — depending upon what office you are running for — meeting the voters and supplicants, having them sign pledge cards, arranging meetings, house parties, rallies, tours and handing out literature.

"This can be phenomenally expensive if it falls upon one financier, but it never does. The lavish show of money attracts more money. The City or State committee will share part of the cost with you if you agree to tack the rest of the ticket to your kite. If the impact of your name is such that a person can hardly turn his head without seeing it, the contractors, suppliers, bankers, insurance agents, the people who will be doing business with the city or state under your administration, will form a line outside your door to contribute.

"The more money you get, the more expansive your campaign becomes, but the money is never squandered. Inevitably you must have a finance or steering committee of hard-boiled and hard-headed men, accustomed to handling money, accountants and bookkeepers who keep track of it. The common belief that a smart operator can pick up a lot of easy money during a campaign is a myth.

"Any substantial contribution to a campaign is in the nature of an investment. The contributor expects to profit in some manner after election. When the impending landslide is apparent, contributors on the other side write it off as a loss and come in with their money. They want to be with the winner.

"When that happens, the opposition often panics. The prototype of the poor but honest candidate of years ago is the desperate contender, outmaneuvered from the beginning, unable to buy television or radio time, newspaper space or the necessary advertising to compete who charges publicly that the lavish use of money in the city or state by the opposition has been scandalous; that leaders have been bribed and blocks of votes purchased and that election laws have been outrageously flouted.

"When he does that, he not only acknowledges defeat and drives whatever money is left into the opposition camp, but he may find himself caught in his own trap. The charge inevitably backfires in a retaliatory countercharge alleging similar violation of election laws or worse." Curley shook his head thoughtfully.

"It's a double-edged sword," he went on, "more likely to nick the clumsy wielder than his adversary. 'Confucius say: "Poor loser who call cops better have clean hands."' Blowing the whistle and crying 'foul' is an old, tired and worn-out device. It rarely works. The candidate with the money has the legal and accounting talent to prove that he is lily pure. Neither charge ever reached a court. Where will you find an Attorney General, or a District Attorney, who has been through the political mill to be elected to his own job, willing to take such a case into the courts?"

Late in the campaign of 1958, Curley was moved into Boston City Hospital and had a room in a wing that had been built during one of his early administrations as Mayor. He had been failing; it was obvious that he could not last much longer. His mind wandered, but during his lucid moments he talked only of the campaign.

Candidates for all Democratic offices came to visit him. They were photographed with him and interviewed as they left the room. Reporters and photographers were on hand maintaining a death watch.

"How's Kennedy doing?" was his question to each visitor even though he was certain that Kennedy could not lose.

Few could tell how he felt when they confirmed his judgment that Kennedy would get a heavy vote. One visitor summed up how he thought Curley felt by shrugging his shoulders and turning his hands palms upward. "He's on his deathbed," he said, "but he'd go all the way down the line for any Democrat, no matter what he thought of him."

Curley died on November 14. His body was moved into the rotunda of the State House to lie in state. His sons Francis and George stood beside the coffin. More than 150,000 persons filed by his bier, among them United States Senator John F. Kennedy.

In her column "My Day" in December, 1958, Mrs. Eleanor Roosevelt recalled that Kennedy had taken no position on Senator McCarthy and went on to imply that the Kennedys had practically bought the spectacular election in Massachusetts by a flagrant misuse of funds in all cities and towns of the state.

In February, 1959, a writing team from Washington came to Boston and visited newspaper offices asking for permission to look through the Kennedy files. They talked to local City Hall and State House reporters and political editors.

"What are you looking for?" they were asked.

"To be frank about it," one of them explained, "we're looking for unfavorable material, something other than evidence of the amount of money that was spent on the election. It is impossible to believe that all of the Kennedys have been paragons of virtue; that none of them ever stepped out of line. They are always presented as something in the nature of a Holy Family."

"I'm afraid," they were told, "that you'll find this city barren ground. You can scour the clippings or talk to the oldest inhabitants, and you won't come up with much."

"There must be something in the background that would indicate that they are human beings; that one or more of them has made a mistake. A big family like that can't go through life simon-pure."

The political editor shook his head. "This one seems to have done it up to this point," he said. "They were trained not to make mistakes. They don't drink. They don't gamble. They were brought up not to make mistakes. They went to the right schools and colleges. They met the right people. They were in the war. They did the right thing by God and country. They married the right men or women. They're all up to their ears in charities and philanthropies. How can you knock them?"

"It isn't a question of knocking them," the writer said. "We're not hatchet men. What we are trying to discover are the things about them that are not generally known. There's a skeleton in every family closet."

"Probably so," the political writer agreed. "This may be the exception to the rule. If there is one here, it is so well hidden that you'll never find it — or if you do, you'll find that you can't reveal it. It will boomerang and public sympathy will be with them."

"That leaves only the money," one of the writers said.

"Right!" the political reporter agreed. "And the only things you can say about that has already been said about them; and about Rockefeller and Harriman. There can be no graft, no corruption. It's their own money. They're not reaching into a public till to take it away from the taxpayers."

"You mean that each of the Kennedy women is as blameless as Caesar's wife, and the men always remain strictly within the bounds of propriety?"

The political reporter shrugged his shoulders and answered, "Apparently so."

"They must live dull and monotonous private lives," the writer observed.

"They hardly have time for private lives," the political

reporter said. "They're always on public view. They've become accustomed to living in showcases."

While the team was researching the Kennedys in Boston, the Senator was on his way by plane to Alaska. Robert was busy with the McClellan Committee in Washington and the rest of the Kennedys were deployed around the country. What could investigators expect to discover about the Kennedys in Boston? The Senator and Robert maintain residences in the city. They spend whatever time they can during the summer at Hyannisport.

The Kennedys are now known as "an old Boston family." They have been in the city for more than a hundred years, among the first of the Potato Famine Irish descendants to acquire that antiquity. The Senator has an office and staff in the Boston Post Office building. He and Robert are rarely out of the public eye.

There is no question that the Kennedys, all of them, are girding for the next Democratic convention, and there is no doubt, either, that if John F. Kennedy is the Democratic nominee for President of the United States, the Kennedys, all of them, will go for broke.